Once Upon a Secret

Once Upon a Secret

*My Affair with
President John F. Kennedy
and Its Aftermath*

Mimi Alford

RANDOM HOUSE
NEW YORK

ISBN 978-1-62090-456-5

Once Upon a Secret

Chapter One

Everyone has a secret. This is mine.

In the summer of 1962, I was nineteen years old, working as an intern in the White House press office. During that summer, and for the next year and a half, until his tragic death in November 1963, I had an intimate, prolonged relationship with President John F. Kennedy.

I kept this secret with near-religious discipline for more than forty years, confiding only in a handful of people, including my first husband. I never told my parents, or my children. I assumed it would stay my secret until I died.

It didn't.

In May 2003, the historian Robert Dallek published *An Unfinished Life: John F. Kennedy 1917–1963*. Buried in one paragraph, on page 476, was a passage from an eighteen-page oral history that had been conducted in 1964 by a former White House aide named Barbara Gamarekian. The oral history had been recently released along with other long-sealed documents at the JFK Presidential Library in Boston, and

Dallek had seized upon a particularly juicy tidbit. Here's what it said:

> Kennedy's womanizing had, of course, always been a form of amusement, but it now gave him a release from unprecedented daily tensions. Kennedy had affairs with several women, including Pamela Turnure, Jackie's press secretary; Mary Pinchot Meyer, Ben Bradlee's sister-in-law; two White House secretaries playfully dubbed Fiddle and Faddle; Judith Campbell Exner, whose connections to mob figures like Sam Giancana made her the object of FBI scrutiny; and a "tall, slender, beautiful" nineteen-year-old college sophomore and White House intern, who worked in the press office during two summers. (She "had no skills," a member of the press staff recalled. "She couldn't type.")

I wasn't aware of Dallek's book when it came out. JFK biographies, of course, are a robust cottage industry in publishing, and one or two new books appear every year, make a splash, and then vanish. I tried my best not to pay attention. I refused to buy any of them, but that didn't mean I wouldn't occasionally drop into bookstores in Manhattan, where I lived, to read snippets that covered the years I was in the White House. Part of me was fascinated because I had been there, and it was fun to relive that part of my life. Another part of me was anxious to know if my secret was still safe.

The publication of Dallek's book may have been off my radar, but the media was definitely paying attention. The Monica Lewinsky scandal, which had nearly brought down the Clinton Administration five years earlier, had stoked the public's interest for salacious details about the sex lives of our leaders, and Dallek's mention of an unnamed "White House intern" lit a fire at the New York *Daily News*. This was apparently a Big Story. A special reporting team was quickly assembled to identify and locate the mystery woman.

On the evening of May 12, I was walking past my neighborhood newsstand in Manhattan when I noticed that the front page of the *Daily News* featured a full-page photograph of President Kennedy. I was already late to yoga class, so I didn't pay much attention to the headline, which was partially obscured in the stack of papers, anyway. Or maybe I didn't want to see it. I was well aware that tabloids such as the *Daily News* tended to focus on all things personal and scandalous about JFK. Such stories always made me queasy. They reminded me that I was not that special where President Kennedy and women were concerned, that there were always others. So I hurried past, pushing the image of JFK out of my mind. Keeping a secret for forty-one years forces you to deny aspects of your own life. It requires you to cordon off painful, inconvenient facts—and quarantine them. By this point, I had learned how to do that very well.

What I missed, in my rush to get to yoga, was the full headline below the photo: "JFK Had a Monica: Historian Says Kennedy Carried on with White House Intern, 19." Inside was a story, taking off from what was in Dallek's book and featuring a new interview with Barbara Gamarekian, who said she could remember only the nineteen-year-old mystery intern's first name but refused to reveal it. Her refusal, of course, only incited the *Daily News* team to dig deeper.

The next morning, at nine o'clock, I arrived at my office at the Fifth Avenue Presbyterian Church, as usual. I hung up my coat, as usual. I took my first sip of coffee from C'est Bon café, as usual. And then I sat down and checked my email. A friend had sent me a message that contained a link to a *Daily News* story. I clicked on it, not knowing what it was. Up came a story with the headline "Fun and Games with Mimi in the White House." He had sent it to me, he said, because of the "funny coincidence" of our names.

For the first time in my life, I knew what people meant when they said they had the wind knocked out of them. I went cold. I quickly closed my door and scanned the article. Though my last name at the time — Fahnestock — was not mentioned, I felt a peculiar sense of dread, that everything was about to change. This was the moment I had feared my entire adult life.

I tried not to panic. I took a deep breath and mentally checked off all the things that *weren't* in the article. The *Daily News* didn't know where I lived. They hadn't contacted any of my friends. They hadn't reached out to people from my White House days. They didn't have my picture. If they had known any more about me they would have included it, right? And they certainly would have tracked me down for a comment.

None of that had happened.

Besides, I had lived through close calls before. A year earlier, the author Sally Bedell Smith had called me at home. She said she was doing a book about how women were treated in the sixties in Washington. It sounded innocent, but it was enough to put me on full alert, and I suspected a somewhat different agenda. I wasn't ready to start peeling away the layers of secrecy and denial yet, certainly not with a woman I'd never met. I said I couldn't answer her questions and politely asked her not to call me again, and she honored my request. My secret was safe.

But this *Daily News* story felt different.

The day after it ran, I arrived at work to find a woman sitting outside my office. She introduced herself as Celeste Katz, a reporter from the *Daily News,* and she wanted confirmation that I was the Mimi in the previous day's story.

There was nowhere to hide, and no point in denying it.

"Yes, I am," I said.

"Mimi Breaks Her Silence," read the headline the next morning.

At this point in my life, I was sixty years old and divorced, living quietly, by myself, in an Upper East Side apartment a few blocks from Central Park. In the early nineties, four decades after dropping out of college, I'd gone back and earned my bachelor's degree at the age of fifty-one. I was a lifelong athlete and a devoted marathoner who spent many predawn hours circling the Central Park reservoir, and enjoying the solitude. My ex-husband, with whom I'd had a stormy divorce, had died in 1993. My two daughters were grown and married, with children of their own. For the first time in many years, I was feeling a measure of peace.

I had spent time in therapy getting to this place, getting to know myself. After being mostly a stay-at-home mom, I had come to take a great deal of pride in my work at the church. I'd worked there for five years, first as the coordinator of the audio ministry (recording and producing the extraordinary sermons of Dr. Thomas K. Tewell, our senior pastor) and then as the manager of the church's website. The audiotapes I produced had grown into a significant source of the church's funding—and the work itself provided not just income but routine and solace. I am not a religious person, but I am a spiritual one, and I loved my work at the church. I also loved my privacy.

When the news broke, it broke everywhere—not only in New York but across the United States and in Europe, too. Here, unfortunately, was my fifteen minutes of fame. The headlines ran the gamut, from predictable to salacious to silly: "From Monica to Mimi." "Mimi: Only God Knows the Heart." "JFK and the Church Lady!" I was mocked by one of my favorite writers, Nora Ephron, on the op-ed page of *The New York Times*. Interview requests poured in, my answering machine full of messages from Katie Couric, Larry King, Diane Sawyer, and, of course, the *National Enquirer*, which actually slipped an envelope of twenty-dollar bills under my apartment door (which I gave to the church). Weekly magazines deluged me with letters. "Dear Ms. Fahnestock," they all began, "I apologize for the intrusion. I know this isn't an easy time for you, but . . ."—and then they got to the point. A Hollywood producer sent flowers before writing about acquiring the film rights to my story; he offered a million dollars in writing before meeting me. Literary agents descended, wanting to represent me. Edward Klein, author of not one but two scurrilous books about the Kennedys, called to say that if I let him ghostwrite my book I'd be rich and would "be able to live in peace." Emails arrived from friends, well-wishers, celebrity stalkers, and critics. A college acquaintance provided some comfort: "Please remember that all of this is 'this week's news,'" she wrote. "It will go away. It's just that JFK is like Elvis. We all think that we know him and we always want to hear more."

I turned down all the media requests. I thanked my well-wishers for their kindness. I ignored the critics, concluding that there was no way to reason with people who thought I was intentionally trampling on JFK's memory or who thought I was making it all up. I reminded myself that it wasn't my idea to go public; going public had been forced upon me.

I had spent the last forty years in fear of being hunted down, found out, exposed. And now that moment had come. But it was unexpectedly liberating. A calmness came over me as the media storm hit full force. I realized I could handle it, that I had nothing to be ashamed of. I was through with hiding.

To the throngs of reporters camped out in front of my apartment building, I handed out a simple statement: "From June 1962 to November 1963 I was involved in a sexual relationship with President Kennedy. For the last 41 years, it is a subject I have not discussed. In view of the recent media coverage, I have now discussed the relationship with my children and my family, and they are completely supportive."

And then I said nothing more.

My full name is Marion Beardsley Fahnestock Alford. In many ways, those three surnames tell you everything you need to know about me and where I come from. I was a Beardsley for the first twenty years of my life, which included the time I was intimate with JFK. I was a Fahnestock for the next four decades, taking the name of the man I married in January 1964, two months after JFK's assassination. Fahnestock is the name attached to the bulk of my adult life and the name my two daughters were born with. I am an Alford now, because of my marriage in 2005 to Dick Alford, the great love of my life, whom, ironically, I would never have met if I hadn't been outed in 2003. It's the only name I go by today, the only name on the jacket of this book.

There's a reason for that. I am no longer the sheltered

nineteen-year-old Mimi Beardsley, who entered into a relationship with the most powerful man in the world. Nor am I the scared, emotionally crippled Mimi Fahnestock who spent a lifetime living with, and struggling to overcome, the consequences of that relationship.

I am Mimi Alford, and I do not regret what I did. I was young and I was swept away, and I cannot change that fact. It's been almost ten years since my secret was revealed to the world, and I've spent a lot of time in the intervening years thinking about this tender episode of my life, and how to express my feelings about it, or even if I should. I don't have such doubts anymore. Until that day in May, there had been an emptiness inside me that I didn't know how to fill. But since then, the happiness and contentment I have come to know as Mimi Alford have freed me — and taught me the importance of taking control of my story.

At first, I wrote letters (never mailed) to my oldest granddaughter, to "set the record straight." "Dearest Emma," I began, "I have a story I want to tell you because someday when you are older there's a chance you might come across my name in a book about an American President. I want you to know the facts. . . ."

But there was so much more to the story than just getting the facts down for the record. Living with a secret had stunted me emotionally, and I realize now that my letters were only tentative steps at understanding. Taking complete control would demand intense self-reflection, and not just beginning and ending with my time at the White House.

This book represents a private story, but one that happens to have a public face. And I do not want the public face of this story — the one where I will be remembered solely as a presidential plaything — to define me.

It may be hard to accept that a chaste teenage girl can end up in bed with the President of the United States on her fourth day in the White House. But no story is as simple as that.

It begins on a train to Washington, D.C.

Chapter Two

It was a hot, muggy Sunday in Trenton, New Jersey, June 1962. The train car I boarded was jammed past capacity and lacked air-conditioning, quickly turning my favorite madras dress into a mass of wrinkles. The air, as it always was then, was thick with cigarette smoke. But none of that bothered me. I was not yet a college sophomore, not yet twenty years old, and here I was, on my way to Washington, D.C., having landed the plummiest of summer jobs—an internship in the White House. The next morning, I would be walking through the West Gate and going to work in the press office of the Kennedy Administration.

Of course, I had very little idea of what this actually meant. I knew some basic things: where I would be living, whom my roommate would be, where I was supposed to show up on the first day of my internship, and who I was supposed to ask for. I knew I was going to wear my favorite madras dress if it survived the train ride, or if I could iron it in time. But beyond that, I had no idea what the job would entail, or whom I would be working with. For that matter, I still had only the foggiest idea of how the internship had fallen into my lap in the first place.

I would soon learn that most people at my level had secured their positions by pulling strings or calling in favors,
even for the lowest-paid internships. Some interns had family connections or parents who were big party donors. That
wasn't me. There were also those who had such a profound
passion for politics, they had landed their jobs through sheer
force of will. That wasn't the case with me, either. I hadn't
even applied for this internship. My knowledge of government was limited to what I'd learned in my freshman poli-sci
classes. If I had a political affiliation, it probably leaned more
toward the moderate Republicanism of my parents, who had
loved Eisenhower and favored Richard Nixon, not John F.
Kennedy, in the 1960 presidential race.

Like many young people in the early 1960s, however, I
was not immune to the star power, and renewed sense of
purpose, that the dynamic President from Massachusetts
represented. He was younger than my father by twelve years.
He was witty and charming and handsome on TV. He had a
beautiful young wife who matched him step for step in style
and glamour. And it was she — Jacqueline Bouvier Kennedy — who, in a roundabout way, had gotten me this job in
the first place. Let me explain.

This wasn't my first visit to the White House. The year before, during my senior year at Miss Porter's — a boarding
school for girls in Farmington, Connecticut — I had served as
editor of the *Salmagundy*, the student newspaper. As it happened, Jackie Kennedy had also attended Miss Porter's, class
of 1947, and, like me, had worked on the *Salmagundy*. As an
aspiring journalist, I had kept my eye on Mrs. Kennedy
throughout the 1960 campaign. She was already our school's
most famous graduate (or "Ancient," as we call them), and if

she became First Lady, it would be a big coup to land an interview with her. I'd write to her and make a formal request. How could she say no to a fellow Ancient?

A month after the inauguration, Hollis French, the school's headmaster, helped me draft the letter, officially requesting an interview for the *Salmagundy*. I typed it on school stationery, sent it off, and spent the next few days—which felt like weeks—waiting for the mail, checking the mail, and being disappointed when the mail contained no response from the First Lady. Finally, on March 10, a cream-colored envelope engraved with "The White House" in dark blue landed in my mailbox. Although I was dying to rip it open on the spot, I ran into Mr. French's study so we could read it together. Inside was a typed letter from Letitia Baldrige, the First Lady's social secretary and chief of staff, and herself a Miss Porter's alum, gently turning down my request. With grace and kindness, Miss Baldrige cited the First Lady's hectic schedule and the "lineup of well over one hundred correspondents and journalists awaiting the opportunity for a personal interview with her."

That was the bad news. The good news was that Miss Baldrige asked if I'd be interested in coming to the White House and interviewing her about Mrs. Kennedy. She even suggested she'd help me assemble some clips to go along with the story. This wasn't your standard brush-off. I was being invited to the White House, if not to speak to the First Lady, then to report on the next best thing: a fellow Ancient who was in the news and had a seat at the table of power. My visit was scheduled for the last week in March 1961, during my spring break.

I flew down a day early on the Eastern shuttle out of La-Guardia Airport and spent the night in Chevy Chase with my

parents' friends, who celebrated my foray into big-time journalism by taking me to dinner at the National Press Club. My
hosts discreetly drew my attention to the well-known names
dining around us. The next morning, I walked through the
White House East Gate a few minutes before my eleven
o'clock appointment.

Miss Baldrige greeted me in her featureless office, where
she was stationed at a very unglamorous, government-issue
desk, surrounded by unpacked boxes (the Kennedys had
moved in only seven weeks earlier). Despite the drab decor, I
felt like I was in the presence of royalty. Miss Baldrige—who
insisted I call her Tish, though that seemed impossible—was
meticulously dressed in a tailored dark wool suit and silk
blouse, the apotheosis of poise and hospitality. (After her White
House years, she would go on to become a bestselling author
of books on etiquette and social manners.) Perhaps she was
merely extending an extra dose of kindness to a fellow Miss
Porter's girl, but Miss Baldrige had clearly given thought to my
visit. She had compiled a stack of clippings about the First
Lady from around the world, secured me a guide, and even arranged for me to meet the President. He was scheduled to
spend time with a group of physically challenged children in
the Rose Garden, she said, and I was meant to join them.

My guide that day would be Priscilla (Fiddle) Wear, yet
another Miss Porter's alum, who had graduated in 1958, the
year before I arrived. Fiddle (a childhood nickname because
she couldn't pronounce Priscilla) was something of a legend
at school because of her job at the White House, but I'd
never met her before. All I knew was that she and her roommate, Jill Cowan, had left Goucher College to work for then
Senator Kennedy on his presidential campaign and both
now had jobs at the White House. Fiddle and Jill were in-

separable. Jill (predictably dubbed Faddle) worked in the press office; Fiddle was an assistant to Evelyn Lincoln, the President's personal secretary.

Fiddle led me from Miss Baldrige's office in the East Wing, and I was immediately impressed (and a little intimidated) by her confidence and professionalism, by the way she navigated the halls so confidently, as if no space was off-limits to her. As we walked, she mentioned that because of spring break, the White House was jammed with tourist groups and friends of friends; this would make it very difficult to get across to the West Wing. So she took me on the scenic route, through a maze of underground tunnels and hidden stairwells, feeling her way along. After a couple of mistaken detours into a kitchen and a laundry, we emerged in the West Wing just outside the Cabinet Room.

Seeing that it was unoccupied, Fiddle opened the door and beckoned me to follow her. I made my way cautiously around the huge wooden table, touching the backs of each of the chairs, imagining all the important decisions and heated debates that took place in this room. It seemed impossible that I was here.

"Wouldn't Miss Smedley be impressed?" I said, invoking the name of Farmington's revered modern European history teacher. Adopting Miss Smedley's grande-dame voice and theatrical gestures, I imagined what she would say if she were with us. "And here is where FDR debated the merits of i-so-*lation*-ism and measured the costs of going to war with Nazi Gerrrrmany. . . ." Fiddle laughed and joined in, and for a minute or two we were back to being schoolgirls, waving our arms like Miss Smedley, playing at an imaginary chalkboard in the Cabinet Room.

Back in the hallway, a woman nearly ran us over as she rushed to the Oval Office.

"That was Dr. Janet Travell, the President's doctor," Fiddle whispered.

I waited for a while by Fiddle's desk, which was a few steps outside the Oval Office, while she went back to her typing. Through a window, I could see Miss Baldrige guiding a group of children into the Rose Garden, which was my cue to go outside and join them. Fiddle turned from her typewriter and escorted me outside, delivering me to Miss Baldrige. Tish motioned for me to stand next to her among the kids. The two of us towered over them as we waited for the President to emerge. This was so much more than I had counted on. Then the doors of the Oval Office swung open, and out into the Rose Garden came the President of the United States.

Of course, I was nervous and starstruck; what high school student wouldn't be? I was curious to see how the real person compared to what I had read or imagined. President Kennedy was taller, thinner, more handsome in person than he looked in photographs. He was patient and charming with the children, shaking hands and talking to each one, crouching down to their level. He was, after all, a politician, the most gifted and successful in the country. Although this was probably just one of many meetings and ceremonial functions on the schedule that day for the President, no doubt promptly forgotten the moment he moved on to the next obligation, he was also keenly aware that the few seconds those children had in his presence would be something they'd remember forever.

When my turn came to shake hands with him, Miss Baldrige stepped in. She introduced me by name and mentioned that I was a student reporter.

"Where do you go to school?" he asked, taking my hand in his.

"Miss Porter's School, sir," I managed to say. The whole thing felt unreal.

A smile of recognition. "What brings you here?" he asked.

"I'm writing an article for our school paper, the *Salmagundy*, about the First Lady."

"Are you a senior?"

"Yes, sir."

"Where are you going to go to college next year?"

"Wheaton or Hollins."

"Well, it's nice to see you," he said. "Good luck."

"Thank you, Mr. President."

And he was gone.

The story I wrote about my experience, "Ancients in the White House," filled almost the entire issue of the *Salmagundy*, and was a great success around campus. On the day it appeared, my classmates were reading it everywhere I looked. I was proud, even more so after I sent the issue to Tish Baldrige, who promptly wrote back: "A charming article — written with the deftness of an Ilka Chase, a Clare Luce and a Mme de Staël, all rolled into one." She was nothing if not an expert in the social graces, a pro at making a teenage girl feel good about herself. I slipped her letter into a photo album my parents had given me.

So when the call came from the White House press office a year later, it seemed to make at least a little sense. The story I wrote, after all, was essentially about the link between Miss Porter's and the White House. Tish must have remembered me and my interest in journalism, awarded me a few bonus points for being part of the Farmington sisterhood, and suggested me for the open position. I'm speculating here, because I never asked or was told *why* I was offered the internship. I only knew that I couldn't say no.

Which was great for me but less so for my father. This sudden opportunity meant he had to make an unpleasant phone call, pulling me out of the summer job that he'd arranged for me as a receptionist-in-training at a New York law firm. I felt terrible about this, and about going back on my word, but he was only too glad to do it. "If it's a choice between interning in the White House and training to be a receptionist in Manhattan," he said, "it's no contest."

I was on my way to Washington.

I grew up in eastern New Jersey in a rambling Colonial farmhouse, one of the oldest in Middletown Township. The main house dated to 1781, with two substantial additions from 1800 and 1850. It had fourteen rooms, including seven fireplaces, a pine-paneled library with the original hand-hewn beams, and a ballroom, a remnant of a more elegant past, which we rarely entered except for birthday parties and Christmas celebrations. My mother named our house Still Pond Farm. "No more moving," she said.

Had I not gone to Washington that summer, I would have commuted one hour by train to midtown Manhattan every day and spent the weekends with my family and friends swimming at the beach club half an hour from our farm, working in the garden with my mother, and helping with chores on the property. My father, a trust officer by day at the Fidelity Union Trust Company in Newark and a gentleman farmer on the weekends, was happiest in his overalls on his tractor, mowing our sixty acres of fields and orchards. When I think of him, I think of him on his tractor, chugging along in the late-afternoon light on warm summer evenings, climbing down only when it was time for dinner.

It was, from all outward appearances, a life of preppie

privilege. I had a sister, four years my senior, whose nick-name was Buffy. I had a brother, Josh, two years ahead of me in school, who was a junior at Princeton, following in the footsteps of our father, after graduating from St. Paul's in New Hampshire. I had another brother, Jimmy, four years younger than I, who would soon be sent away to prep school in Rhode Island and then on to Princeton. My sister Deb, six years younger than I, would be attending Miss Porter's in a couple of years. And, yes, we wore a lot of plaid.

All the WASPy and preppie boxes were checked, and yet I didn't feel, growing up, that we were excessively privileged. This was due in large part to my mother. She was epically, virtuosically frugal. She would never consider hiring a carpenter or painter or other craftsman to fix something if she could do it herself. By the time I was eight years old, when we left New York City for the farm in New Jersey, I was well aware of my mother's "I'll-do-it-myself" ethos. It was impossible not to be. As her first project in our new home, I had watched her steam off the old, peeling wallpaper in every room, patch the walls, and paint them herself. Then she tackled the fading slipcovers and curtains, buying fabric and sewing new ones. She built bookcases and refinished old pieces of furniture; she scraped and painted all the wooden shutters; she made circular felt skirts for my sisters and me with appliquéd scenes from Currier and Ives; she drove endless car pools, cheered us on at all our school games, cleaned the house, cooked our meals, and tended the chickens and sheep on the farm (the animals were not pets but sources of food, though my siblings and I could never stomach the notion of eating the lambs that grazed on our property). She was a dynamo of energy and self-sufficiency, with a domestic skill set that would have made Martha Stewart proud.

This was how she was programmed to behave. Her ambition in life had been to get married, raise a brood of well-mannered children, free her husband of any duties that might interfere with his all-important career, create a happy, comfortable home, and manage the family finances so that we never spent more than we had. In this she wasn't much different from other moms in our neighborhood and across America at the time, although I suspect she was an extreme version of the species.

My mother was an attractive woman of above-average height (5'7") with delicate facial features, a slender silhouette, perfect posture, and short brown wavy hair. Everyone called her Liddy, which seemed to suit her. She was friendly and outgoing, and could display the silky, upbeat charm of a hostess when required, but more often than not, she carried herself with an air of seriousness and heavy responsibility. She was rarely frivolous, although I do remember her going on silly diets—such as eating only bananas for a week—every now and then. The diets were pointless; her inability to sit still practically guaranteed that she would never be overweight. (At one point her father, who had a farm nearby, hired a cook for us because he was worried that she was working herself into exhaustion. The cook departed within the month when we learned that she was draining my father's gin bottle and refilling it with water—and my mother, to our delight, resumed cooking all our meals.)

My father, Randy, was a large, jovial man—with big ears, a big nose, and a big, ready smile. I do not have a single photo of him in which he's not smiling, laughing, or being playful. But behind that smile lurked something darker, something that only later, in the sixties, would be diagnosed as manic depression. As young children, we didn't see much evidence of his sadness and despair, largely because in his lowest moments my mother would take over and cover for him. Those were very difficult years for her, but I don't think she had a single moment of regret for choosing this man as her partner—and vice versa.

My parents had been married for thirty-six years when my father died suddenly of a heart attack in 1973, at the age of sixty-eight. He had always loved hats, and after he died our mother put together a collage for each of his children with photographs of him in his favorites. I still have it hanging in my office today.

If I'm making our home in New Jersey in the 1950s and early '60s sound like an idyll of rural gentility, that's because it felt that way to me at the time. I found happiness there and learned to love being alone. In what strikes me now as admiring mimicry of my mother's domestic dynamism, I devoted hours, as a young teenager, to playing with a massive but elegant wooden Victorian dollhouse that rested on a table in my bedroom. I electrified it, painted the rooms, hung wallpaper, and decorated it with store-bought period furniture, always to scale. I was engrossed in every detail, not only technically but emotionally. I populated the dollhouse with an imaginary French family—a couple named Marie and Paul Perot, with three children—for whom I created elaborate backstories and life crises. As I made up situations and dialogue for them, I would move them around from floor to floor, room to room. Devoting my spare hours to that dollhouse was liberating; it gave me a sense of control. My French family had to obey me, not the other way around.

If this was rebellion on my part, it was of the most private kind. It suited my personality. I sometimes think I was born with an internal governor on my emotions, set permanently between medium and low. I didn't question my parents, and would never dream of speaking back to them. I rarely fought or even argued with my brothers or sisters. I think I was too afraid of confrontation and its consequences.

We inhabited a self-contained world where nearly every phase of our lives was mapped out for us, defined by the expectations of our so-called class. My sisters and I curtsied as children and always rose when an adult walked into the room. We were taught that every kind gesture required a thank-you note in return. We said grace at every family meal and "passed love" around the table by holding one another's hands and squeezing in turn. We heeded the implicit agreement that politics or religion was never openly discussed, for fear of causing offense. Money was a taboo topic; it was distasteful to mention how much one made or spent on anything, and wealth was definitely not something to be flaunted. It was assumed that everyone we knew was a Republican and shared the same Protestant faith.

We were constantly reminded that self-reliance was the greatest virtue. We each had a schedule of chores on the farm that went beyond making beds and maintaining tidy rooms. My job was to keep the border of the flower garden weeded and neatly trimmed. When major disasters struck, such as a septic field destroyed by flooding, we all grabbed shovels and buckets to help our mother and father rebuild it.

Most important in our family was where we went to school. It was simply assumed that we would attend one of the prestigious boarding schools that my mother and her siblings attended: Miss Porter's, St. Paul's, St. George's. Education was a virtue, but this went beyond virtue: Having one of these schools on your résumé was like a shorthand embedded with status and significance.

The Social Register, the annually published volume listing prominent families in New York, was a fixture on my mother's desk. I don't recall my parents consulting it religiously—not like the comic figure of Sir Walter Elliot at the beginning of Jane Austen's *Persuasion,* who "never took up any book but the Baronetage"—but it surprises me now to admit how important that book was in my parents' circle.

There was no more status-significant event in my youth than being "introduced to society." Since we had lived in both New York City and New Jersey, my mother insisted that my sisters and I make our "debuts" in not one but two states. This decision was motivated by good intentions on her part—she wanted only the best for us—but it was a nerve-testing experience for me. It wasn't that I minded getting dressed up in a long white silk dress with white kid gloves up to my elbows. It was that these debutante balls, universally derided as "cattle shows," required the presence of young men as our escorts. Meaning: I was obliged to invite one or two boys of my acquaintance and a boyfriend as well. My problem was that, by my eighteenth birthday, I was on a run of bad luck—or I should say no luck—with boys. The ones I took a shine to tended to look past me, to the girls who were a little more, well, girly. If I had carved out an identity for myself at this point, it was as an athlete. I'd been captain of the field hockey team and the basketball team at Rumson Country Day School and was such a fast runner in track that I'd run on the boys' team against the fathers on alumni field day—and won. Hardly an asset when it came to dating.

My greatest, and only, success in the boy department had been gaining the notice of Louis Timolat when we were both in the eighth grade—and letting him kiss me. Once.

And that was the last kiss anyone bestowed on me through high school.

So I didn't have a boyfriend for my New Jersey debut at the Rumson Debutante Ball of September 1961, which took place at the Seabright Lawn Tennis and Cricket Club. I had asked two brothers of Farmington friends, who graciously agreed to be my escorts. They were perfect gentlemen during the evening, but it didn't shock me that their overriding agenda was to meet other girls there. I had also invited two of my brother's classmates from Princeton, but they considered me a kid sister from the start and ignored me all night. I can recall all this with bemusement rather than malice now, but at the time, the petty slights stung. It was a hot, sticky, uncomfortable evening, and my dominant emotion, the one I remember all these years later, was disappointment.

My coming out in Manhattan took place three months later at the Junior Assemblies in the Grand Ballroom at the Plaza Hotel. My escort this time was my older brother, Josh, whose smashing appearance in white tie and tails seemed to ensure that he would dance with every girl *but* me. I consoled myself with the memory of another dance where Josh, in full brotherly prank mode, danced with me but dangled a five-dollar bill behind my back to entice other dance partners to cut in and take me off his hands. This time, at least Josh had the good manners to spare me from that embarrassment.

It's a wonder I didn't rebel against the whole humiliating experience — or by extension, against my mother, for putting me through it. But it wasn't in me to question or protest. I was the dutiful daughter, yielding to my family's prerogatives and expectations.

There are many reasons why I had so much trouble with boys during this time in my life. For one thing, at 5'9", I was taller than many potential male suitors. I was also skinny. There's this awkward dead zone in many a tall girl's development, before she has filled out, when she is trapped between being coltish and being just plain goofy. That was me at fifteen. (It's also why I picked up the nickname "Monkey"—all arms and legs.)

For another thing, I was sent off to Miss Porter's when I was fifteen. Attending an all-girls school, to be sure, makes it difficult to get to know boys. The 220 girls at the school were as cloistered as you could get without taking vows. When I was a student there, in the dark ages of 1958 to 1961, no boy could come near the school except on Saturday afternoons— and even then, only if a girl had signed him up as her "caller" *a week before.* The arrangements had to be made by mail because we were not allowed to receive or make phone calls. (The only allowable phone conversations were with our parents, no more than once a week.) If callers were willing to clear that hurdle, they then had to deal with a series of protocols seemingly designed to strip all the romance out of a date. When the callers arrived, they were met by Miller, the school's longtime uniformed guard, who checked their names against a list. If it all checked out, the girls and their callers were then restricted to walking around the mile-long Gundy Loop and forbidden to stop, lest sinister behavior such as hand-holding ensue. You could measure the intensity of a couple's relationship by how long they walked: the most ardent couples took as many as four or five loops. When the walking was over, the girls would escort their callers to the headmaster and headmistress's house for the obligatory cup of tea. After that the boys departed, back to their rooms at Groton and Deerfield and Taft.

With all the daunting, labor-intensive planning required to gain entry onto our campus and the limited scope of activities during the actual visit, it's amazing that any boys were willing to make the trek to our school at all. It's not as if they arrived to find us at our prettified best. Our wardrobe did nothing to distinguish us: We heeded the unofficial uniform of cardigan sweaters over boys' button-down shirts and wool kilts over knee socks. Our shoes had to be Abercrombies, sturdy brown lace-up leather shoes with fringed leather tongues.* We accessorized with a standard kit—a barrette to hold our hair in place, a gold circle pin, a string of pearls— and we weren't interested in makeup, not even lipstick, which caused the townspeople who saw our pale faces at church on Sundays to fear that we had influenza.

I didn't take to Miss Porter's immediately. The first six months there, I was so homesick I spent much of my free time looking out my window at the cars going by and praying that one of them would be my father coming to take me home. It didn't help that we lived in big houses, not dormitories, which reminded me of what I'd left behind in New Jersey and made my homesickness worse. I was intimidated by my classmates, especially those from New York City, who seemed so smart and worldly and grown-up. My classmates were trained to be kind and decent to everyone, including new girls like me. If there was any intimidation, it was all in my insecure mind. I'd been something of an athletic star at Rumson Country Day, but at Farmington I had to start all over again from the back of the pack. I didn't have the good sense, at that point in my life, to know that things would get

---

*I made the mistake of enrolling at Miss Porter's sporting saddle shoes—which caused me a ridiculous amount of psychic pain. My mother, ever observant, must have seen this, because she was responsible for one of my signature moments of joy as a teenager when she gave me a pair of Abercrombies for Christmas my junior year. Shoes, then as now, were obsessive totems of happiness for many women. I wasn't immune.

better. I knew only that during my first six months there, I felt anxious and lonely and unsure of myself. For the first time in my life, I felt like I didn't belong.

I dealt with my budding self-esteem issues in a peculiar but not unusual way: I stopped eating. For some reason, I was haunted by the image of a girl I'd known in New Jersey who, after three months at boarding school, had returned for Christmas vacation thirty pounds heavier. I didn't want to be that girl. The more anxious I became, the more fixated on that girl I became. I spent a lot of time in front of the mirror, wondering if I was getting fat. When I wasn't ignoring food or shunting it aside, I lived on the whites of hard-boiled eggs because I had read that the yolks contained all the calories. As a result, I came home at spring break nearly thirty pounds lighter than I had been at Christmas.

My mother was horrified—I had been slender all my life, but now I was downright skeletal—and immediately took me to a doctor in New York, who was a close friend of our family's. He talked to me in wise, soothing tones, without a hint of condescension, about loneliness and my lack of close friends, and my feelings of inadequacy. I don't remember the word *anorexia* ever coming up. He explained that I wasn't powerless to deal with these issues; they were within my control. As lost as I was, that made sense to me.

I returned to finish the year emotionally revived. I started eating, I started regarding my classmates as friends rather than competition, and I started feeling like I could hold my own. I found comfort in all the conformity. For my remaining two years there, I focused on my studies and put my energy into extracurricular activities such as the drama club known as Players, a reading club called the Myopians, and the *Salmagundy*, where I managed the small staff and was responsible for making sure the paper got out on time. When I graduated in 1961, it made a certain sense to me that our class poll hailed me as "Changed Most Since Sophomore Year." But it was a big surprise to be designated along with two classmates as "First Woman President."

If there was a gap in our otherwise first-class education, it may have been that few of us seriously considered a career at the time of graduation; instead, we looked forward to marriage and raising a family. I don't blame the school; it was purely a function of the times. When I started the next phase of my education as a freshman at Wheaton College, an all-girls liberal arts school in Norton, Massachusetts, I didn't feel like I was being prepared for life with a steady paycheck. I was looking forward, like my friends, to getting married to a suitable young man with a pedigree not much different than mine. True, I'd had a bad run with boys, but I'd blossomed out of my coltish phase. And I was hopeful.

When I look at snapshots of myself from that time, I see a tall, slim, athletic girl who had finally gained some social confidence. I wasn't shy with boys. I could talk and flirt and parry with them easily. I just needed to find someone who understood me.

That was the girl I was in 1962, staring out the train window on my way to Washington, D.C. I was educated and poised but also innocent, naïve, with no sexual experience, and (like all but the most worldly of nineteen-year-olds) oblivious to anything that didn't immediately affect me. As the steamy, overcrowded train car clattered along through Philadelphia and Baltimore, my biggest worry was that I had already sweated through my favorite cotton madras shirtdress and would have to find something else to wear for my first day of work. I felt better knowing that my mother had also packed me two drip-dry shirtdresses from the Johnny Appleseed catalogue. They would be perfect work clothes in the swampy climate of a Washington, D.C., summer.

In other words, my only worry in the world was about what to wear.

When the train arrived in Washington's Union Station, I carried my one suitcase to the curb and hailed a taxi to the house I would share with a family friend named Wendy Gilmore, who was working at the State Department. The house was more like a bungalow, but it was in the heart of Georgetown on O Street.

Wendy was twenty-five and instantly welcomed me as if I were a younger sister. That first night, we cooked supper together and then went over a map of the best bus routes to the White House. I tried not to show my nervousness about the job. I wasn't thinking of the glamour or the prestige of working at the White House or how much luster the internship would add to my résumé, if indeed I was ever to have a résumé. I was just anxious about showing up on time and doing a good job. I called my parents to let them know I'd arrived safely, and went to bed early.

The next morning, as I skipped down the front steps of the house in my Pappagallo flats and my freshly ironed madras dress, I considered hailing a taxi just so I could savor the thrill of telling the driver, "1600 Pennsylvania Avenue, please." But that foolishness passed quickly. I kept my money in my pocket, walked to the corner, and caught a bus to the White House.

Chapter Three

"Mimi Beardsley," I told the guard when I arrived at the West Gate. I was trying very hard to seem professional.

He checked his list.

"Would that be . . . Marion Beardsley?" he asked.

"Yes, that's me," I said.

"Okay, you can go through," he said, and once I was past him, I let out a sigh of relief. On the bus ride over, I had worked myself into a frenzy, convincing myself that my internship was a mistake or a cruel joke—and that I would be barred from entering the White House. Such are the insecurities of a teenage girl; sometimes you feel like a fraud or an interloper, that you don't belong.

My relief at being let through didn't last long, however. My next challenge was finding the press office without getting lost. I walked up the path to the main door of the West Wing and entered the White House. I crossed the reception hall where reporters liked to loiter on the off chance they could grab an interview with high-profile people exiting the Oval Office, and stopped. I had no idea where I was going, so I asked a guard for help. He smiled and directed me down a short hall to the left.

I was hoping that Fiddle would be there to greet me, but she was nowhere in sight. In fact, the first person I encountered was Pierre Salinger, the President's press secretary, who brusquely waved me into his office. Although he was only thirty-six years old, Salinger was already a larger-than-life figure in the nation's capital, as well as a media darling.* He had been Kennedy's press secretary during the presidential campaign and had been the obvious choice for the same role in the White House. He was short, slightly paunchy, and a bit of a clotheshorse, although the net effect was often more rumpled than elegant. He was rarely seen without a cigar in one hand and a clutch of papers in the other. He didn't have the Ivy League panache or patrician reserve that defined the Kennedy inner circle, but he was both cultured (he had been a child prodigy at the piano in his native San Francisco) and street smart. It was Salinger who had been so impressed by Kennedy's quick-witted seduction of the media that he prodded the President to conduct his news conferences live on television — something that no president had dared before. His main job then, as it is now for press secretaries, was to control and occasionally pacify a restive White House press corps that never got as much access to the President as it wanted. He had a glorious, rich baritone that could not be contained by office doors or walls, which is precisely what I heard in his office as he paced back and forth, punching the air with his arms, barking out orders to two men who stood at the side of his desk. They were dressed just like him — sharp gray suits, crisp white shirts, thin ties. They turned out to be his assistant press secretaries, Malcolm Kilduff and

---

*In October 1964, when he ran for the Senate in California, *Time* magazine put him on the cover.

Andrew Hatcher. Mr. Salinger introduced me to them as the new summer intern, and then sent them on their way.

He turned to me and spelled out my immediate duties.

"See those teletype machines?" he said, making a show of opening the bathroom door and steering me inside. I'd never seen a teletype machine before, and I was confused about why four of them were in the bathroom, two against a wall and two in a bathtub. They were clattering away, spitting out steady streams of paper from the Associated Press, United Press International, Agence France Presse, and Reuters.

"It's the noise," he said, intuiting my confusion about why they were in the bathroom.

Then he pointed to a set of clipboards hanging on a wall in his office. My job, he explained, was to cut the streams of teletype paper into foot-long sheaves and clip them onto the boards, one for each news agency, before they overflowed onto the floor.

His final instruction was to call him Pierre.

Then he dismissed me, saying, "The girls will show you the rest."

The "girls" he was referring to were the secretaries in the open room outside his office—serious, determined women, most in their thirties, who had no problem being referred to as "girls." I didn't have a problem with it, either, to be honest. The word *feminism* had not yet entered my vocabulary. This kind of dynamic seemed to me to be the natural order. The men were in charge. The women assisted them.

Christine Camp, Pierre's executive secretary and the de facto leader of the office's female staff, continued my White House initiation. I spent the next half-hour filling out employment forms in order to collect my sixty-seven-dollar-a-week salary—before taxes. Then she ushered me to a standard gray desk just inside the press office door. This desk would be mine, she told me, and so would the clunky gray Remington typewriter alongside it. There was a telephone, the standard black rotary model with a half-dozen flashing buttons at its base, for me to use. For someone who had never worked in an office before—the only jobs I'd ever had were as a babysitter and a mother's helper—it felt like a whole new world of possibilities was opening up. The idea of having my own desk, and my own typewriter, in the White House press office, made me suddenly feel like I'd arrived. I tried my best to act normal, but this wasn't normal. It was all so incredibly exciting.

I had a feeling I wasn't alone in this. Everyone around me seemed to be executing the nifty trick of appearing simultaneously hyperactive and relaxed. They seemed to glow with delight at being part of something special. That feeling quickly washed over me as well, and for perhaps the first time in my life I, too, began to feel special. I began to feel a sense of purpose.

Chris Camp explained that one of my jobs was to answer the press office phone—and she made it clear that there was an art to dealing with these calls. If it was a routine question from a reporter—for example, what time Pierre Salinger would be holding a press briefing in his office—I was free to provide the information. But if it was remotely substantive—ranging from a reporter wanting clarification on an Administration policy or merely checking a quote—I was to immediately transfer it to someone more senior. I would have to learn to juggle six blinking lights—six different lines, ringing constantly—without disconnecting anyone. It wasn't rocket science, but I didn't sleep so well those first few nights, until I'd mastered the system.

In all, there were nine people in the press office, seven of us jammed into the tight open space, and Pierre, who luxuriated in a roomy office with two doors, one of which opened into our room, and another of which opened into a hallway that led to the Oval Office. (I later learned from Pierre's memoir, *With Kennedy,* that some evenings the President would venture into our quarters from the Oval Office to snoop around our desks. The President had a habit of borrowing books and documents, which Pierre would then have to retrieve from his night table.) The atmosphere was remarkably open and casual; in such tight quarters, it had to be for anything to get done. Pierre himself, despite the sensitive nature of his job, rarely worked behind closed doors, which allowed me to hear the telex bells ringing away in the bathroom. Wire services such as UPI had bells to signal important incoming messages: four bells meant an urgent message; five bells was a "Bulletin"; ten bells, a "Flash," was reserved for the most important news. A ringing bell was my cue to jump up and collect the wire copy for Pierre.

You could figure out the "girls'" seniority by our proximity to Pierre's office. Because I was newest, my desk was farthest away, by the door. Jill Cowan, Fiddle's close friend, had a desk facing mine. Jill had the title of secretary, but it was never clear to whom she directly reported. Helen Ganss, a permanent fixture on the press office staff dating back to the Truman Administration, sat just outside Pierre's office. Chris Camp, my boss, sat literally inside Pierre's office. There were small file cabinets and a bookcase crammed along the wall. Off to the left was the doorway to another room, which Andy Hatcher and Mac Kilduff shared, along with their secretaries, Barbara Gamarekian and Sue Mortensen Vogelsinger.

Pierre conducted twice-daily news briefings in his office, where the reporters would crowd in, simulating the crush, as

Pierre liked to say, of a jam-packed New York subway car at rush hour. There was a tremendous sense of energy in that room, of always being in a hurry, of trying to stay on top of the dozens of things that were happening at once. Everyone pitched in. It was an incredibly invigorating place to work, a buzzing hive filled with smart, bright people.

On my second day, I received a promotion. Barbara Gamarekian put me in charge of the press photography file. One of her responsibilities had been to escort the press photographers in and out of the Oval Office during bill signings, and to identify the congressmen and senators and other special guests who attended the events, for captioning when the photos were eventually printed. But she'd fallen behind and badly needed help. "I'm so busy that I haven't had time to sort out the files and they're a mess," she said. "Could you do that?"

I didn't hesitate to say yes. This, at last, was something I actually knew how to do. I had become a pro at filing and cross-referencing at the *Salmagundy*. I realize now that Barbara was following the time-honored tradition that governs all summer internships: You smile nicely and dump on the interns all the mind-numbing or labor-intensive tasks you don't want to do. But I didn't mind. I loved looking through all the photos and learning the names of the people posing with the President. I was astonished at how much of his daily routine involved photo opportunities.

The casual atmosphere in the press office, where all the men removed their jackets and rolled up their sleeves and everyone called one another by their first names, seemed to exist everywhere in the White House, even at the front gates. When Jill Cowan took me to lunch my first day, the guard marked us out and remembered I preferred to be called

Mimi, not Marion, my given name. There were no cement barricades blocking the various entrances as there are now, and cars drove right past the entrance on Pennsylvania Avenue. The White House and everyone in it back then were just so much more accessible. On that first day, as Jill and I sat at a counter at a nearby coffee shop, picking at our egg-salad sandwiches and talking about everything *but* politics and government, we could have been tourists ourselves, wandering around the capitol sights, not people who worked a dozen yards outside the Oval Office.

But even though the atmosphere was casual and relaxed, I wasn't. I was worried about doing a good job and petrified of messing up. At some point during that lunch, I had a minor panic attack, imagining that the news wires were churning out streams of paper that were strewn all over Pierre Salinger's bathroom floor, and that I was going to be fired. I took a last bite of my sandwich and convinced Jill that we had to hurry back. After all, I wanted to be the kind of worker who gets invited back next year.

That first week was hectic and exhausting in the best possible way. The President was taking a trip to Mexico soon to meet with President Adolfo López Mateos, and everyone in the press office was working on logistics—who would be on the advance team, which press members would go, where they would stay, where to set up a temporary press office, on and on. Reporters were constantly coming in and out, nodding to the new face as they passed by my desk. Jill introduced me to some of them—people such as Merriman Smith from UPI (who would later win a Pulitzer Prize for his coverage of the President's assassination) and Hugh Sidey, who covered the White House for *Time* magazine. They were always in sight, always angling for a newsy tidbit or asking to set up interviews.

The office favorite had to be NBC's Sander Vanocur, who was relentlessly charming and regularly plied the staff with boxes of glazed doughnuts. For a young woman who had been editor of her school paper, these men were heroes.

White House staffers also drifted in and out of the press office. I remember one of them, Wayne Hawks, who arranged transportation for reporters and staff, stopping by my desk after a meeting on the upcoming Mexican trip. He already knew that I came from New Jersey, and he told me he had gone through officer training during World War II at Fort Monmouth near our farm, and we sat and talked about New Jersey for a while. I was startled, some time later, to read about our meeting in the *Newark Evening News* in a section titled "Washington Footnotes." My mother clipped the little story and sent it to everyone in the family. "Mimi Beardsley of Sleepy Hollow Road is adding a decorative note to the office of the White House press secretary, Pierre Salinger. . . ." it said. I can only surmise that Wayne Hawks had planted the story with someone in the press corps as a highly nuanced attempt to sway some future votes in Monmouth County, perhaps in the midterm elections or when the President ran for a second term.

I couldn't get over the fact that everyone—from the front-gate guards to the travel office people—seemed to know me by name, even though we had never been formally introduced. It was as if I had been awarded membership in an elite club without ever having to go through the initiation process. Even as an intern I was immediately made to feel a part of the team. Looking back on it now, that was the most extraordinary feeling I can recall from those first days: I felt like I belonged.

Chapter Four

By my fourth day at the White House, I was feeling considerably more comfortable with my teletype duties. I no longer woke up at night, worrying about failing to respond to a ten-bell incoming message, or walking in to a mess of paper on the bathroom floor. That morning, I was cutting up a sheaf of clips just before lunchtime when my phone rang. I hurried to my desk and picked it up.

"Want to have a swim?" asked a male voice on the other end of the line.

"Who is this?" I asked, though the voice sounded familiar.

"It's Dave Powers."

Dave Powers was one of the President's closest aides. I had met him the day before, when Jill spotted him in the hallway and called him in to introduce me. Smiling and full of good cheer, Dave welcomed me like a long-lost friend. Like Wayne Hawks from the travel office, he seemed to think it was of enormous geopolitical significance that I came from New Jersey—and made a point of letting me know that he knew all about me. He knew I had two brothers and two sisters, and, ever playful, announced that a paltry passel of five children was insufficient to qualify the Beardsleys as a good Catholic family. (He ignored the fact that we were actually Episcopalian.) An Irish Catholic himself, he admitted to falling short of expectations even more dramatically because he had only three children. Our encounter was little more than run-of-the-mill joshing, but it had all the components that leave an impression—the flattering awareness of me and my family, the self-deprecation about his failure to breed more children, the creation of that inclusive, almost intimate, feeling that he and I had something in common—and make you remember a person's voice even after one meeting.

Now he was on the telephone, asking me if I wanted to take a midday swim in the White House.

A swim?

I suppose my first thought should have been to question the propriety of this invitation, not to mention how incongruous it was. Dave may have known details about my life, but he didn't know me. Swimming is something one does with one's friends and family. People don't automatically jump into bathing suits with strangers, and certainly not at their brand-new workplace.

I suppose I should have carefully considered all this, but I didn't. In retrospect, I was thrown off balance. My first response to Dave, which I suppose was my best stab at expressing my confusion, was, "Where do we swim?" I didn't know the White House had a pool. He assured me it did, a hundred yards or so from the press office.

My second response was more to the point: "I have nothing to wear."

"Don't worry about that," Dave said, adding, "There'll be a couple of other staffers there. And we have lots of bathing suits. You'll find one that fits. I'll swing by the press office in a few minutes and we can walk over." Then he hung up, as if the matter was settled.

I stared at the handset for a few seconds before I placed it back in its cradle, befuddled by the invitation. Then I looked at Jill's desk, hoping for guidance. Is this normal? I wanted to ask. Does this happen all the time? But she wasn't there. I thought about my mom and dad and how I should be keeping a list of all the amazing things I was seeing, so I could tell them later. I thought about how lucky I was to be here. I pictured their astonishment when I would call them that evening to describe my White House swim.

I never did make that call.

Within minutes, Dave Powers arrived in the press office to escort me. He greeted me warmly and kept up a cheerful patter as we followed the covered colonnade that bordered the Rose Garden and led to the entrance of the indoor pool. He again mentioned that I wouldn't be alone. He didn't seem at all discomfited by the circumstances—a private swim in the middle of the day with a young woman he didn't know.

Dave's official title was special assistant to the President; unofficially he was known as the First Friend. His roots with the President went back to the first Kennedy campaign for Congress in 1946, when Powers's considerable people skills helped the wealthy candidate connect with Boston's blue-collar voters. He followed Kennedy to Washington, D.C., and never left his side through three terms in the House, one term in the Senate, and now as leader of the free world. *Newsweek* referred to him, not unadmiringly, as an "irrepressible leprechaun," and he placed his mischievous charm at the President's disposal. No one was more loyal to the President or more in his thrall. When Kennedy and Powers toured the West Wing together for the first time, Powers compared the moment to "being Alice in Wonderland . . . He looked ten feet tall to me, and he seemed to grow every day." With the President's blessing, Powers had carte blanche in the White House; he could go anywhere and say anything. (He was notoriously irreverent. It was Powers who, while walking the shah of Iran into the Oval Office, patted the potentate on the shoulder and said, "I want you to know you're my kind of shah.") Above all, Dave Powers's job was to make the President happy.

As we reached the entrance to the pool, Fiddle and Jill suddenly appeared by my side. They seemed to be veterans of this swimming ritual, which instantly put me at ease. I had not seen Fiddle since she had given me a tour of the White House the year before. I was hoping that she and I would become great friends when I arrived for my internship, but she was four years older—practically a generational divide among college-age girls like us.

I followed the girls into the dressing room, where, as Dave had promised, there were more than a dozen bathing suits hanging on hooks. They were plain one-piece cotton suits of varying sizes, with boxer shorts and gathered fabric at the bustline. I wondered to whom they belonged, or if they were left there as public property to be used whenever someone had the inclination to get some exercise. Fiddle and Jill didn't waste any time wondering; they just started stripping down and leaping into suits. Their enthusiasm was contagious, so I reached for the first suit at hand. The fit wasn't as snug as I would have liked, but it wasn't in danger of falling off when I hit the water, either.

The White House pool, long since covered over to create today's press office and briefing room, was a perfect oasis, designed to simulate a tropical island. The walls on three sides of the pool were painted with floor-to-ceiling scenes from St. Croix in the U.S. Virgin Islands, with palm trees swaying in the breeze and puffy sailboats moving through turquoise water. The murals had been a gift, orchestrated by Mrs. Kennedy, from the President's father, Joseph Kennedy. The fourth wall was mirrored, so the space felt vast, and you were completely enclosed by the faux warmth and sun. As I walked past the mirror toward the edge, I stole a glance at myself in the borrowed suit and felt a wave of relief. I may not have had a lot of curves, but at least I had good posture, and my long legs played up my height and slimness.

Dave Powers joined in as well—sort of. He took off his shoes, rolled up his pant legs, and sat on the edge of the pool, dangling his feet in the water. I boldly dove in, eager to feel the refreshing splash of cool water on my body and to join Fiddle and Jill, who were already floating around, chatting and giggling. But the water wasn't refreshing at all; it was as warm as a bathtub. Later I learned that the temperature was always set at ninety degrees at the President's insistence—to soothe his chronic back pain. I remember treading water with Fiddle and Jill, asking them whether the sandwiches and drinks left by the side of the pool were meant for us, when President Kennedy walked in.

He was standing above the three of us in the pool, handsome, tan, in a suit and tie.

"Mind if I join you?" he asked.

Fiddle, ever confident, said, "Our pleasure, Mr. President."

Off he went into the dressing room, only to reemerge

minutes later in a pair of dark swimming trunks. He was remarkably fit—flat stomach, toned arms—for a forty-five-
year-old man. Fiddle and Jill didn't seem the least bit
surprised to see him, which confirmed to me that this midday swim was a usual event for them and, hence, perhaps not
as strange as I had thought.

The President slid into the pool and floated up to me.
"It's Mimi, isn't it?" he said.

"Yes, sir," I said. "Mimi Beardsley."

"And you're in the press office this summer, right?"

"Yes, sir, I am," I replied.

"Is Pierre treating you all right?"

"Yes, Mr. President. He seems very nice."

"What's he given you to do?"

I told him about collecting the wire stories and answering the phone and sorting out the press photographs.

"I hope some of that will be interesting," he said. "You
have a good place to stay for the summer?"

"Yes, sir. In Georgetown. My roommate works for the
State Department."

"Well, nice to see you, Mimi," he said, and he floated
away toward Fiddle and Jill.

I spent a few more minutes circling the pool, not knowing exactly what to do, and swam over and chatted for a while
with Dave. Then the President climbed out of the water—
which Dave took as our signal that the swim was over. I
grabbed a quick bite from the food tray, since the pool esca-
pade had become my lunch break, changed out of the wet
suit, and returned to my desk.

There, in the tight quarters of the press office—among
the closely knit group of women who had been working at
the White House since the Administration's first day—the effect of what I had just done began to dawn on me. Suddenly

I felt self-conscious, as if everyone knew where I'd been and was staring at me with stern disapproval. It wasn't exactly hard to figure out: My hair was wet and smelled of chlorine. It must have been obvious that I had been swimming, but none of my co-workers said a thing. I wasn't about to bring it up, either. Who would believe it? And what would they think?

This special access would hardly have endeared me to my office mates. It was the rare employee inside the White House who did not gauge her status by how much contact she had with the President—or even if the President knew her name. Barbara Gamarekian, for example, claimed she had worked on Kennedy's campaign from the beginning and had been in the White House for a year and a half before the President ever addressed her by name. She admitted as much in her oral history at the John F. Kennedy Presidential Library: "I can remember going back to the office and sort of floating on a little pink cloud, saying to everyone: 'He knows my name! He knows my name!' " she'd said. Now, here I was, the summer intern moving to the front of the line, leapfrogging career women who had labored long and hard on the presidential campaign to get a sought-after job at the White House. So I kept my head down and my mouth shut and went about my work as if nothing had happened.

My hair was still damp when my phone rang later that afternoon. It was Dave Powers again, asking if I would like to meet everybody after work at five-thirty for a welcome-to-the-staff get-together. This was impossible to turn down.

"Where do I go?" I asked.

"Upstairs," he said. "I'll pick you up."

I didn't know what "upstairs" meant, exactly, but I had enough sense not to ask any of the other women in the press office—in case they weren't included in the invitation. I wanted them to like me, or else I would have to endure a very long summer.

My initial wish was that Dave had given me more notice so I could have washed my hair and put on a nicer dress, but it would have to do. As the workday drew to a close, I kept my eye on the other women in the press office to see if they were going to the ladies' room to brush their hair or put on lipstick, but they were sticking to their routine; nothing unusual was happening.

When Dave appeared at my desk, I felt intensely self-conscious, convinced that curious glances were being thrown my way by everyone in the office, and perhaps they were.

For the second time in a few hours, I followed him to an unfamiliar part of the White House. Dave was humming quietly to himself as we walked. The White House is not a simple building. It is a warren of offices and odd hallways and large public spaces spread out over four floors and two basements. The West Wing, with the exception of the Oval Office and Cabinet Room, is surprisingly claustrophobic—and represents a small fraction of the White House's total space. Dave ushered me through the winding corridors past the Cabinet Room, then outdoors under the West Colonnade and past the entrance to the swimming pool, then inside again and down a wide hallway to an elevator.

When the elevator door opened on the second floor it finally dawned on me that I was standing in the family residence. It was a grand, elegant space, an oasis of calm in a very busy building. I wanted to pause for a moment to take it all in, but Dave kept going, leading me to an area known as the West Sitting Hall. It was lined with bookshelves and comfortable couches and chairs in front of an enormous half-moon window opening out on the western sky. There I found Fiddle and Jill in conversation with a man named Kenny O'Donnell, who was the President's appointments secretary and a Kennedy loyalist on a par with Dave Powers. O'Donnell was the dark, serious foil to Powers's court jester. The President valued both of them enormously, but for different reasons.

"Have a daiquiri," Dave said, lifting a frosted pitcher from the coffee table and pouring me a glass. I hesitated. I was not much of a drinker.

"Thanks," I said, accepting the glass with a polite sip.

"Welcome to the White House staff," Dave said, raising his glass, almost making it sound as if this cocktail hour was staged solely to honor my arrival at the White House.

"It's great to be here," I managed to say.

I drank down the daiquiri and, feeling a little more relaxed, did not protest when Dave filled my glass again. I may not have been an experienced drinker, but I knew enough to eat some food. I plunked myself down in a chair by the puffed cheese hors d'oeuvres on the coffee table—and listened in on what Jill and Fiddle were discussing with Dave and Kenny. Among the more interesting tidbits I overheard was the news that Mrs. Kennedy and the two children, four-year-old Caroline and eighteen-month-old John John, had left for Glen Ora, the house the Kennedys rented in Virginia, where the First Lady kept her horses.

Suddenly, everyone rose to their feet, as if "Hail to the Chief" had begun to play, and into the room walked President Kennedy. I'm not sure why I was surprised to see him for the second time that day. After all, he *lived* here. But I had gotten so caught up in my daiquiri, it slipped my mind that he might show up.

The President greeted us, took off his suit jacket, sat

down on the couch, and put his feet up on a coffee table. I could feel the center of gravity in the room shift immediately. We stopped talking among ourselves and turned ever so slightly toward the President, making him the center of attention. He was, no doubt, aware of this; it must have happened to him dozens of times a day.

I savored the idea that I had been included in the President's most trusted White House circle, those with whom he chose to relax and take a break from the relentless responsibilities of the day. Honestly, it was thrilling. I felt as if someone had pinned a medal on me or that I had been tapped to join the most prestigious club at school. But I was also uncomfortable. Despite the good cheer in the room and the overwhelming glamour of being on the second floor of the White House, a space very few people ever get to see, I knew I didn't belong to this group. I hadn't done anything to earn it. I didn't know if I should stay or go. I kept my eye on Fiddle and Jill, and determined I would leave when they did.

Then the President rose from the couch and walked over to the chair I was sitting in. "Would you like a tour of the residence, Mimi?"

A private tour of the White House from the President of the United States. This was an extraordinary invitation. Mrs. Kennedy had made it her highly publicized mission to restore the White House's tired and drab interiors. On her own, she had raised money and persuaded wealthy contributors to donate prized art and furniture to restore the White House to her vision of understated elegance. I had been interested in design since the moment I was given my dollhouse at thirteen. I was well aware of Mrs. Kennedy's efforts. The invitation was impossible to resist.

As I stood up, the daiquiris went immediately to my

head. I looked around, tipsy, expecting the entire group to join us for the tour. But no one else moved. Of course not, I told myself. They're always up here. They know every room by heart.

President Kennedy was already leaving the room, and I followed after him, as if pulled by a magnet. He opened the first door along the hallway, explaining that it had once been a guest bedroom, which Mrs. Kennedy had converted into the family dining room. Standing with the President in the doorway, I tried to take in the newly installed antique wallpaper panels, decorated with scenes of the American Revolution. But I got the sense that the President had done this tour many times before and was in no mood to linger. He then led me across the central hall and opened another door, stepping aside for me to enter.

"This is Mrs. Kennedy's bedroom," he said.

That was odd, I thought. Her bedroom? Where did *he* sleep? It was a beautiful room, decorated in a light powder blue with floor-to-ceiling windows overlooking the South Lawn. The bed, with a draped canopy, was really two beds — a hard mattress for the President, because of his back, and a softer one for the First Lady. There was a sitting area in front of the fireplace with a small white couch. Together we looked out the window in the fading June sun.

"Beautiful light, isn't it?" he said. I agreed. He walked me through the personal memorabilia in the room: a pastel of Caroline, a terra-cotta bust of a young boy.

I noticed he was moving closer and closer. I could feel his breath on my neck. He put his hand on my shoulder.

"This is a very private room," he said.

The next thing I knew he was standing in front of me, his face inches away, his eyes staring directly into mine. He placed both hands on my shoulders and guided me toward the edge of the bed. I landed on my elbows, frozen halfway between sitting up and lying on my back. Slowly, he unbuttoned the top of my shirtdress and touched my breasts. Then he reached up between my legs and started to pull off my underwear. I couldn't believe what was happening. But more: I couldn't believe what I did next. I finished unbuttoning my shirtdress and let it fall off my shoulders. He pulled down his pants and then he was above me.

He paused briefly when he felt some physical resistance.

"Haven't you done this before?" he asked.

"No," I said.

"Are you okay?" he asked.

"Yes," I said, and he resumed, but more gently.

"Are you okay?" he kept saying.

I nodded, propped up on my elbows.

After he finished and hitched up his pants, he smiled at me and pointed to a door in the corner.

"There's the bathroom if you need it," he said.

I gathered my underwear off the floor and my dress off the bed. I was still wearing my bra but nothing else as I walked across the room to the bathroom.

When I came back he was no longer in the bedroom.

"I'm out here," he called, from outside in the West Sitting Hall, where our evening had begun. I walked out to join him—he was sitting on a sofa—and looked around to see if anyone else was there, but the residence was empty. It was just the two of us.

I was in shock. He, on the other hand, was matter-of-fact, and acted as if what had just occurred was the most natural thing in the world.

"Would you like something to eat?" he said. "The kitchen's right here."

"No, thank you, Mr. President," I replied.

What I really wanted to do was leave, and he must have sensed that. He asked where I lived, made a phone call, and then explained that a car would pick me up at the South Portico entrance. He showed me to the private elevator.

"Good night, Mimi," he said as the door opened. "I hope you're okay."

"I'm fine, Mr. President."

Downstairs, a guard showed me to the South Portico, and there, as promised, was the car to take me home.

Chapter Five

It was still early in the evening on the third Thursday in June 1962, a few days before the summer solstice, the longest day of the year. Through the rear window of the town car, I could see the White House reflecting the golden hues of the setting sun, and could make out the lights through the windows of the rooms in the second-floor residence. As we drove out of the gate, I thought to myself, *I was just up there. With the President.*

I wasn't being wistful or self-congratulatory or smug. I had looked back to assure myself that what had happened had, in fact, happened, that I wasn't dreaming.

It wasn't a dream.

I quickly turned back and stared straight ahead as the driver glided through D.C. traffic. I was oblivious to the government buildings and tourist sites passing by, lost in my own head, trying to make sense of the previous two hours, to piece the events together so that my moments with the President could be understood as . . . what? Inevitable? Enjoyable? Unusual? Incomprehensible?

At nineteen, I didn't have the ability to connect the dots

into a narrative that made sense. So I focused on the most obvious truth: I wasn't a virgin anymore. It kept echoing in my head: *I'm not a virgin anymore.* I had always imagined that my first time would be with the man I loved on my wedding night. I wasn't "saving" myself out of religious or moral conviction. This belief was simply the conventional — and widely accepted — ethos among girls my age. And I was as conventional as anyone I knew.

But the circumstances surrounding my "first time" were hardly conventional. Not even in my most florid imaginings did I think it would be with an older man — let alone someone of my parents' generation. Let alone the President of the United States.

How did I get myself into this position?

I reran the scene in the residence, recalling the laughter around the living room and the giddy effect of the daiquiris. Nothing in the scene suggested an air of sexual intrigue or menace. In recalling it, I tried to locate Fiddle and Jill, but they remained on the margins, out of the picture. I tried to locate Dave Powers but he, too, was stubbornly hidden from view. The only lasting image was that of the President in his shirtsleeves with his feet propped up on a coffee table. He was incredibly handsome and commanding and alluring.

That's what I felt as I gathered my thoughts in the back of the town car: I had been overwhelmed by the presence of the President.

Wendy Gilmore wasn't home when the town car pulled up at my door, which was a small relief. I didn't want to face her, in case she asked me about my day. It wasn't that I was afraid of breaking down in front of her, I was simply exhausted and wanted to be alone. I went straight upstairs to my bedroom and looked at my face in the mirror. It didn't look any different. I hadn't been transformed from "girl" to "woman" in an evening. The smell of the President's 4711 cologne still clung to me, so I stepped into the shower. As the hot water washed over me and I looked down at my body, I had the thought that other women of my generation who were shielded from knowledge about their own bodies must have had: *So that's sex?* I didn't know if it had been good, bad, or indifferent. I didn't know if it was meant to be slow or fast. I didn't have an opinion about it being "caring" or "meaningful." I had nothing to compare it to.

As I toweled off, I continued to retrace my actions from the day. I reexamined the impulse behind Dave Powers's suggestion for that lunchtime swim. Had he orchestrated the whole thing to give the President a chance to look me over? And what about Fiddle and Jill? Were they somehow involved as well?

At the time, I didn't have the stomach to try to answer those questions.

I've wrestled over the years with other questions about that day. I've wondered why the small group in the residence left after the President took me on the tour and whether they knew what was going to happen in the bedroom. I suspect they did. I've wondered, too, about the unsolicited offer of my internship and why I'd been invited to work in the White House in the first place—was it because the President had a thing for Farmington girls? He'd married one, after all, and there were Farmington graduates scattered all over the White House. The truth is, I'll never know.

One thing I didn't wonder about is whether I had led him on or in some way seduced him. On the face of it, that was laughable. My skills as a seductress were so nonexistent that the thought of intimacy between us didn't occur until after the intimacy had begun. As I say, I was incredibly sheltered and naïve. But there's no doubt that up there in the residence, I was the direct object of *his* skills at persuasion. He was a man adept at—and accustomed to—getting his way. He had that politician's gift of making you feel that when you were in his company you were the most important and interesting person in the world. After all, here was a man who, just months before, had mesmerized the nation with his personal style and glamour, his quick wit, and his élan.

All of which makes me wonder if I could have resisted him. It's a germane question, and my honest answer to it is "No." When we were in the bedroom, he had maneuvered me so swiftly and unexpectedly, and with such authority and strength, that short of screaming, I doubt if I could have done anything to thwart his intentions.

I don't say this to excuse my passivity at that moment— because, frankly, I don't think I need an excuse. I'm not ashamed of what I did. I'm just trying to make sense of it now, fifty years later.

I'm also not trying to make excuses for President Kennedy. He was, no doubt, a charmer, a seducer, an insatiable lothario, as I and everyone else would eventually learn, each in our own time, some more quickly than others.

In sharing the details of that night with others, I always get the same reactions about President Kennedy's behavior. At first, the response comes in the form of dismay—at the President's sinister intentions. "You *must* see it, Mimi," they say. "You were set up! He was a predator!" Then, when I don't agree, the response changes to disappointment—in me. Others take the argument a step further. They are not shy about bringing up the R word—*rape*—to describe what happened to me. I don't see it that way.

That night, in the midst of my shock and confusion, I felt for the first time the thrill of being desired. And the fact that I was being desired by the most famous and powerful man in America only amplified my feelings to the point where resistance was out of the question. That's why I didn't say no to the President. It's the best answer I can give.

There was a moment, right after the President realized I had never had sex before and was in some discomfort, when he became more tender and solicitous, more aware of me, and I actually felt close to him. I wouldn't describe what happened that night as making love. But I wouldn't call it nonconsensual, either.

Chapter Six

The next morning, I walked into the White House trying to affect a casual manner, as if I didn't have a care in the world. It was the only way I could mask my profound sense of dread that everyone in the press office would intuitively know what had happened the previous night up in the residence. I was particularly anxious about running into Fiddle and Jill. What would they think? What did they know? They were playful and carefree young women who were extremely comfortable in the President's company — and vice versa. Would they regard me as an interloper who had overstepped her bounds or would they greet me with knowing smirks? I wasn't sure which would be worse: their resentment or their approval.

It turned out my dread was misplaced. As I walked into the office at nine o'clock sharp, everything was normal, nothing out of place. There were no glares or knowing glances. Two of my colleagues, who had arrived a few minutes before me, were already at their desks, removing the covers from their typewriters. They said hi to me and went right back to what they were doing. Pierre Salinger wasn't in his office. The whole scene was oddly, eerily quiet, which reminded me that it was a Friday in summer—and people had other priorities besides being chained to their desks. In general, most people in the White House tended to observe a nine-to-five workday—which is funny, when you think about it now. They arrived on time and, unless something urgent was afoot, clocked out at a decent hour, well before the sun went down. Although everyone I saw in the West Wing worked hard and the offices crackled with energy and brisk conversations, it was a far cry from the all-consuming chaos I would later see in TV shows such as *The West Wing,* where staffers pulled all-nighters and tended to charge rather than walk down hallways while arguing about a congressional vote count or some ominous Bureau of Labor statistic. Exciting as the JFK White House was, it wasn't Hollywood-level intensity by any stretch of the imagination. Not in those days.

All of which reminded me of my insignificance in the scheme of things. I was a summer intern, a shadow off in a corner, clipping teletypes and manning phones, hardly on anyone's radar. Any apprehension about my experience with the President becoming an issue at work was purely in my mind—because I was not taking up any space in anyone else's mind.

And I surely wasn't on the President's mind, either.

A week or so earlier, he had endorsed his brother Ted for his old Senate seat in Massachusetts. Ted had just turned thirty that February, the minimum age to be a U.S. senator, and would soon find himself in a tough primary fight against Massachusetts attorney general Edward McCormack, who had powerful Washington, D.C., connections of his own; his uncle John McCormack was the newly installed Speaker of the House. Ted's campaign was being run out of the White House and occupied much of the President's attention. In the meantime, he was also trying to walk a fine line on the issue of civil rights, fending off pressure to sign an executive order prohibiting racial discrimination and to introduce a national voting rights act. He had made health care for Americans sixty-five and older one of his Administration's top priorities, and his signature program—called Medicare— was about to go through three weeks of intense Senate debate before being voted down, 52 to 48. And, of course, there was the perennial focus on reviving the economy, avoiding a recession, balancing the budget, controlling inflation, and appeasing American business's need to know that the President was pro-business. The Dow Jones Average had hit a low on JFK's forty-fifth birthday, which inspired the business press to call it the "Kennedy Crash."

In short, there were quite a few pressing issues occupying the President's attention in early summer 1962. I had no illusions that I was among them.

That Friday morning, I settled in at my desk and lost myself in the tasks at hand. When I overheard one of my co-workers say that the President would be joining the First Lady at Glen Ora for the weekend, a wave of relief washed over me.

I remember that weekend more for what I *didn't* do than for what I did.

I didn't call my parents.

I didn't call my older sister.

I didn't see any friends.

I didn't talk to my roommate, Wendy, who, thank goodness, was away that weekend.

Which isn't to say that I spent the weekend hiding or feeling sorry for myself. When I'm anxious, I organize. So I spent the weekend doing my laundry, cleaning the kitchen,

mopping the floor, cleaning the tub, and restocking the refrigerator. I went shopping for a few items to dress up my
tiny, spartan bedroom. I went on several solitary walks
through Georgetown, losing myself in its maze of beautiful
streets.

My anxiety peaked late Sunday night as I was laying out
my wardrobe for work the next day. Standing over the bed,
considering my options, it struck me that I had no idea what
to expect from this job. I thought I had gone to work at the
White House to learn, to see major-league journalists at
work. And my first three days in the press office met those
expectations. But the events of Thursday night had changed
things forever. I was confused. I couldn't make sense of the
place or the people in it or my role there—and for a brief
moment on that Sunday night, I decided I didn't want to go
back.

The feeling passed as quickly as it appeared. I reminded
myself to be brave, and then crawled into bed.

Week two at the White House began calmly enough. I still
hadn't seen Fiddle or Jill in the office since my encounter
with the President, nor had I heard from Dave Powers. I was
keeping my head down, going about my duties on Monday
morning, when I overheard someone say that the President
had returned from Glen Ora, and that Mrs. Kennedy had
stayed behind in Virginia. The mere mention of his name
jolted me. I sat at my desk, paralyzed, my eyes focused on the
phone. What if it rang and it was Dave? How would I deal
with that? What would I say?

It's odd to me now, almost fifty years later, that I felt this
way, that I still hadn't made up my mind about what I'd say if

he suggested another afternoon swim or drinks in the residence. Frankly, I couldn't decide what I wanted to do. I
couldn't settle my mind. I wasn't revolted or appalled by
what had happened, and I wasn't harmed. I was certainly
confused. Probably the most accurate description of my state
of mind was *fascination*. Being singled out by the President
made me feel special, which was not a feeling I was accustomed to. A story was unfolding in front of me—with me in
a starring role—and I was searching for the answer to the
universal question: *What happens next?*

I prayed that the phone would not ring.

Then the phone rang. It was Dave Powers. "Would you
like to come for a lunchtime swim?" he asked.

I believe that all life stories have at least one pivot point,
a central, animating event from which other events unfold. If
you had asked me to name my pivot point before I started
writing this book, I would have answered with the births of
my daughters—because those two events brought me so
much joy. But I realize now that a pivotal moment isn't necessarily the most joyful or memorable one; it is often just the
moment that reverberates most powerfully.

I realize now that Dave Powers's call, which lasted all of
fifteen seconds, was my personal pivot point—because everything would have been so different if I had simply said no.

But I didn't say no.

I didn't know Dave or the President well enough, at that
point, to appreciate that I had a choice—that I could turn
down the invitation, and all it implied, without repercussion.
It wasn't as if Dave would become petulant or vindictive because an intern said no to an afternoon swim with his boss.

I would eventually come to know that President Kennedy wouldn't have given my absence from the pool that afternoon more than a second's thought. He might have been momentarily disappointed or puzzled, but then he'd have moved on. He wouldn't have punished me for my decision. He was a kind and thoughtful man, beloved by all the people who worked for him. He had true grace when he dealt with people. He would have been incapable of telling Dave Powers to deal with me in some punitive way.* He could be sharp and tough, but he saved such displays of power for people who threatened his presidency or his political agenda, not for people who worked for him. I was no threat to him.

But what's important is what I believed at the time. I believed if I said no, my dream of a full-time job at the White House would slip away forever. I would never again be invited into the President's inner circle. I would never again experience the heady feeling of being in the same room with the President.

So even though I cringe now, I understand why that nineteen-year-old girl said yes to Dave Powers's invitation. She was on her own for the first time in her life, away from parents and siblings, home and school. She was flattered by the repeat invitation. She was determined to have fun, damn the consequences.

---

*Ted Sorensen, JFK's gifted speechwriter, wrote the following about JFK in his 2009 memoir *Counselor:* "His only notable weakness as a boss was his reluctance — indeed, his inability — to fire anyone. Instead he promoted them. . . . I first discovered this Kennedy shortcoming back in the Senate when JFK told me that Evelyn Lincoln — the most loyal, devoted, hardworking, and totally trustworthy member of his team — did not have the intellectual capacity to handle his increasingly important telephone calls and correspondence, that he had tried firing her, but that she kept showing up at her desk every day anyway. . . . JFK kept her on, took her to the White House, and continued to value her loyalty."

That's why I got up from my desk and walked to the pool.

Fiddle and Jill were already in the water, swimming circles around the President. He was floating on his back, letting the warm water work its magic, and trading jokes with Fiddle and Jill. He barely acknowledged my arrival, betraying no hint of what had happened between us just a few days before. I couldn't bring myself to look him in the eye. But I was there in a bathing suit at poolside, wasn't I? What did I think was going to happen? I slid into the pool and floated toward the group. The President now turned in my direction, and seemed genuinely happy to see me, but he stuck to banal small talk. He asked me if I had a nice weekend, if I was enjoying my job, nothing more interesting than that. If he was feeling any remorse or guilt about the last time we were together, he wasn't showing it.

This, in hindsight, was shrewd behavior—and no doubt instinctual for someone so naturally attuned to other people. He created such a feeling of normalcy at the pool that I gradually began to relax. The President didn't touch me or treat me differently or do anything improper, which gave me some comfort. Maybe our previous encounter had been a onetime occurrence and wouldn't happen again. I'm not sure why I believed this, because I'm not sure I can say that I didn't want it to happen again. The truth is, I was deluding myself, behaving like a girl who protests at a boy's advances but complains even more loudly when he stops. So when, later that afternoon, Dave called again and asked me to come up to the residence after work, I accepted. I also assumed that Fiddle and Jill would be there.

But the sitting room was empty when Dave escorted me upstairs. The same pitcher of daiquiris was on the coffee table, right next to the same platter of cheese puffs, and a few minutes later, the President arrived. He and Dave joked back and forth while I held on to my hope that more company was coming. When Dave stood up to leave, I panicked and stood up to leave with him, but the President intervened.

"Stay for supper, Mimi," the President said. "The kitchen staff always leaves food in the icebox."

I froze.

"And have another daiquiri," he said.

Soon he was leading me into a bedroom he hadn't shown me before. It turned out to be his. "Would you like to take a bath?" he asked, showing me into the bathroom. "You can close the door." I was in such a state of nerves that a nice warm bath actually sounded relaxing. "I'll meet you in my bedroom," he said, and left me alone.

This was the beginning of our affair.

Although the President maintained a crowded, highly choreographed schedule, he had to carve out time to tend to his ailing back at least once a day. This forced him to become a creature of habit. The midday swim in the overheated pool was an inviolable part of his routine, and so it became part of my routine as well. I would swim with the President at noon or near the end of the workday, race back to my desk, and then wait for a call to come upstairs in the evening. The governing factor behind these calls, of course, was the presence—or, more accurately, the absence—of Mrs. Kennedy in the White House.

In late June 1962, after the President and First Lady returned from a state visit to Mexico—we all called him "El P" for a week after the Mexican citizens had cheered him as "El Presidente"—Mrs. Kennedy departed on a long trip, first to Hyannis Port with the children, then to Italy for most of August. Alone in the White House for much of that summer, the President called for me at least once, and often twice, a week.

After that first night, we never went back to Mrs. Kennedy's bedroom. We stayed in his, which wasn't as pretty but had a lovely antique four-poster bed with a patterned blue canopy and a seating area with two blue chairs in front of a working fireplace. There were piles of books, newspapers, and magazines scattered about.

As we spent more and more time together, the absurdity of our relationship, and my self-consciousness, gradually began to wear off. The President was particularly deft at defusing any awkwardness about the gross imbalance in our relative status by openly referring to the fact that I was a student—and having some fun with it.

"What did all you girls do locked up in that boarding school?" he often asked.

Of course he was looking for a scandalous answer, but really there wasn't one.

"Nothing," I'd reply, and mean it.

This was an answer he refused to accept. Part of him seemed to be still an adolescent teenager at Choate, and it may have been that I reminded him of a much simpler, easygoing time in his life. He always seemed quite boyish and relaxed when we were together. As time went by, he was also more attentive, more gentlemanly than he had been in our first encounter. There was nothing abrupt in his manner anymore. As our relationship continued through the summer, sometimes he would be seductive. Sometimes he was playful. Sometimes he acted as if he had all the time in the world. Other times, he was in no mood to linger. Our sexual relationship was varied and fun.

President Kennedy was a sensualist. We spent an inordi-

nate amount of time taking baths during our evenings together. He changed his shirts as often as six times a day, as he
hated feeling sweaty or grimy. In that first summer, we turned
the elegant bathroom off his bedroom—with its thick white
towels, luxurious soaps, and fluffy white robes, embossed
with the presidential seal—into our own mini-spa. The only
discordant note were the rubber ducks, which appeared later
that fall, around the time when Vaughn Meader's comedy
album *The First Family* was the number-one-selling record in
the country.* Evidently, after Meader in one skit had the
President listing which toys are Caroline's or John's and
then insisting, "The rubber duck is mine!" a friend sent him
a team of yellow rubber ducks, which he immediately installed as permanent fixtures along the rim of his bathtub.
And every time he saw the ducks, it kick-started a playful
side of him. That was part of his charm: He was a serious,
sophisticated man with extraordinary responsibilities and
yet he was willing to be completely silly, to play along with a
joke at his expense. It was an irresistible quality. We named
the ducks after his family members, made up stories about
them, and often set them racing from one end of the tub to
other. Forty-five years later, after my secret was out, I described these rubber ducks to a friend. "You didn't have an
affair with the President," she concluded. "You had a play-
date."

After our baths, we'd have a light meal—usually cold
chicken, shrimp cocktail, or roast-beef sandwiches, whatever
the staff had stocked in the kitchen refrigerator or left out on
a wheeled-in serving table. I can't recall one time when the

*Meader's LP sold more than 7.5 million copies, still the top-
selling comedy album of all time. You could hear it on the radio, in
dorm rooms, and in living rooms wherever you went that season.

President and I sat down to a hot meal in the residence; for obvious reasons, he would ask the staff to provide food and drinks for him and then give them the night off. Evidently, he felt he could trust his private life with Dave Powers and Kenny O'Donnell and his valet George Thomas, all three of whom appeared to have total, all-hours access to the residence. The Secret Service agents tended to remain downstairs, rarely venturing to the second floor.

We had the full run of the second floor to ourselves, but we rarely ventured beyond his room and the kitchen. He taught me how to scramble eggs the way he liked them, slowly stirring them in the top of a double boiler.

At some point in the evening, he would put a record on the turntable that was built into the wall of the passageway that connected his room to Mrs. Kennedy's. He loved popular music, and his taste tended toward anything by Tony Bennett or Frank Sinatra. It wasn't music that I could relate to. I preferred pop tunes about lovesick girls, like Little Peggy March's "I Will Follow Him" and the Shirelles' "Will You Love Me Tomorrow." About the only place where our musical tastes overlapped was with "I Believe in You" from the Frank Loesser musical *How to Succeed in Business Without Really Trying*. The President would pull out the LP of the original cast recording and set the needle on the big tune from act two of the hit show.* Something about Robert Morse crooning the lyrics — "*You have the cool, clear eyes of a seeker of wisdom and truth*" — seemed to light up some pleasure center deep inside his brain. He liked the song so much I made a point of learning the lyrics so I could sing along.

Sometimes, if it got too late, I would sleep over with the

---

*It won the Pulitzer Prize for Drama in 1962.

President, which seems incomprehensible to me now, given the level of media scrutiny. But at the time, it seemed perfectly natural.

"Do what you want," the President would say to me. "You can go home or you can stay."

On the nights I stayed over, he'd lend me one of his soft blue cotton nightshirts to wear. In the morning I might wake up to the President having breakfast in bed, while reading the many newspapers he had delivered to the residence daily. Then he'd take a bath, where he shaved to save time, get dressed, and head off to the Oval Office between nine and nine-thirty.

I never felt I had to sneak out of the residence in the early hours before the staff arrived. On the contrary, I felt comfortable lingering there with or without the President. The Secret Service agents knew I'd spent the night with the President. Mr. Thomas always greeted me kindly but was too discreet and loyal to ever hint—through a word or a knowing glance—that he disapproved of my presence. I usually went home to change my clothes before coming back to work, but sometimes I just took the elevator downstairs, walked along the portico, past the swimming pool and the Cabinet Room, and into the press office. I was so pleased with myself at being chosen by the President that I didn't feel self-conscious at all about wearing the same clothes two days in a row. If my office mates noticed, I didn't care. I felt invulnerable, as if I were cloaked with the President's power.

During that first summer with the President, I developed what I believed was a close friendship with Dave Powers. It was impossible not to like Dave. He had an Irishman's easy way with conversation, combined with the discretion of a priest. I felt that Dave had an avuncular interest in taking care of me and making sure I didn't get hurt. I realize now that he was creating a smoke screen like a skilled political operative. Dave wasn't taking care of me. He was taking care of the President. I've often wondered how Dave, given my youth and the fact that he had two daughters of his own, rationalized his role as a go-between. The two of us spent a lot of time together in the residence, drinking daiquiris and waiting for the President, but I don't recall him ever once bringing his children up. Doing so would have meant jolting me out of my feelings of being cared for, of belonging. His job was to accompany me upstairs, stay with me for a few minutes, and leave. I often took a long bath and waited for the President in one of the bathrobes.

On occasion, Dave would come back later in the evening, have a drink, and regale us with stories and political gossip. The two men enjoyed each other's company immensely— and sometimes their attention would turn to me. For example, neither Dave nor the President could believe I wasn't the object of universal pursuit by boys my age.

I finally dealt with their incredulity, which was no doubt exaggerated for my benefit, by telling them about Jimmy Robbins, a student at the University of Pennsylvania whom I had dated briefly during my freshman year at Wheaton. *Date* was too strong a word for what we did. Our "romance" consisted of one weekend at Penn, a visit to my home in New Jersey, and a weekend at his parents' house in Bedford, New York, where, it quickly became clear, he much preferred playing golf all day to being with me. As I sat around waiting for Jimmy on Sunday afternoon, his brother took pity and treated me to lunch. But I didn't tell the President and Dave all that; I let the possibility that Jimmy and I were still an item linger in the air.

They both pounced on it, especially the fact that Jimmy was attending the University of Pennsylvania. It inspired a running joke whenever I was around the two of them. "Dave, make sure the Secret Service knows that if a guy shows up to take a tour in a UPenn sweatshirt, to tell him the White House is closed." Or: "You know that guy in the UPenn sweatshirt, Mr. President? We arrested him today."

They were mocking me in the most gentle way, and I glowed because of their attention.

Of course, I wasn't aware at the time that I wasn't unique, that there were other women in the President's life. I never made the logical leap that if he behaved this way with me, he was probably doing the same with others. I would read later that Dave Powers cautioned many presidential lovers to remain silent because such clandestine behavior might become an issue of "national security," but he never mentioned such a thing to me. He didn't have to. If I'd spoken to anyone about our relationship, I figured, I would be revealing my own questionable behavior as well as betraying the President.

I'm hardly the first person to write about the incredible pass the media gave the President when it came to his private life—it's almost unfathomable, given the climate today, when even the most private moments in our public figures' lives are held up for our scrutiny. A big reason, beyond it just simply being a different, more discreet era, was that the media—not all of them, but most of them—worshipped President Kennedy. There were some halfhearted inquiries about the President's indiscretions along the way, though I don't know whether they were about me or the others. Thirty years later, in an interview with the *Washingtonian* magazine, Pierre Salinger would recall how easily he dispatched one such caller.

"I gave him a 1960s answer, not a 1990s answer," Pierre said. " 'Look, he's the president of the United States. He's got to work 14 to 16 hours a day. He's got to run foreign and domestic policy. If he's got time for mistresses after all that, what the hell difference does it make?' The reporter laughed and walked out. That was the end of the story."

My theory now on how the President managed to hide his activities from many of the people closest to him in the White House is that he was a genius at compartmentalizing. As Ted Sorensen wrote in his 2009 memoir, *Counselor:*

> *Throughout our years together, there was a dichotomy in our relationship. I was totally involved in the substantive side of his life, and totally uninvolved in the social and personal side. Except for a few formal banquets, we never dined together during the White House years. The times we were together socially over the eleven years we worked together were few enough that I can remember each one.*

As Kennedy's chief speechwriter, Sorenson supplied the JFK "voice." He knew how the President's mind worked and could brilliantly articulate his beliefs and dreams better than anyone. But even this man, who judged himself second only to Bobby Kennedy in his access and value, never dined with the President alone, never really saw him beyond office hours.

Sorensen's words made perfect sense to me. The President's compartmentalizing allowed him to effectively segregate people in all the areas of his life, one from the other. There was a compartment for his wife and children. There was a compartment for the sprawling Kennedy clan that gathered at the family compound in Hyannis Port. There was a compartment for his inner circle of advisers. There was a compartment for his friends. There was a compartment for members of the press, many of whom felt he was just as much their friend as the object of their reporting. And most obviously, there was a compartment for his girlfriends. His genius was in limiting how often these various compartments overlapped. As Sorensen put it, "I do not remember everything about him, because I never knew everything about him. No one did. Different parts of his life, work, and thoughts were seen by many people—but no one saw it all."

All of which is why it seems plausible that so few people who claimed to know him knew about the extent of his womanizing. The President was in total control of who was invited into his world and what they were permitted to see. But it must have been exhausting.

The President's strategy even kept me guessing about the extent of his relationship with Fiddle and Jill. Did the President sleep with one or both of them, too? The First Lady certainly had her suspicions about Fiddle. "This is the girl who is supposedly sleeping with my husband," she once said (according to Barbara Gamarekian's oral history) in an uncharitable aside, spoken in French, to a reporter from *Paris Match* as the two of them toured the West Wing and came upon Fiddle at her desk. But I had no idea if it was true. If I had suspected anyone in the White House had been in the same boat as I, it would have been Fiddle. I adored Fiddle. She was always poised, always saying the right things. She greeted me with enthusiasm whenever we met, treating

me as if I were her younger sister. Despite her cheerful, playful persona, she was as discreet as a CIA agent. We talked a
lot—mostly about clothes—but I cannot recall one instance
where she revealed a single piece of information about the
President. Although Fiddle—and Jill, too—had an easy relationship with the President and were regulars at the noon-
time swims, more than that I cannot say.

A telling example of how aggressively President Kennedy tested the limits appeared in Sally Bedell Smith's *Grace
and Power*. In the second week of June 1961, she reported, the
President's back problems flared up to the point that his
physician, Dr. Janet Travell, ordered him to take four days off
in Palm Beach, Florida, so he could soak in the saltwater
pool at the estate of a wealthy friend, Paul Wrightsman, and
rest. There with him were the President's close friend Chuck
Spalding, Dr. Travell, the White House chef Rene Verdon,
and a few staffers, including Fiddle and Jill. Among the press
corps that followed President Kennedy everywhere was *Time*
magazine's White House correspondent, Hugh Sidey. As
Sidey recalled it, Kennedy invited him to a big dinner one
evening in Palm Beach, where Spalding, Fiddle, and Jill were
also present. It was a "weird night," according to Sidey, with
the President holding forth, telling jokes and wild tales in
the most unguarded manner. When dinner ended, Sidey offered Fiddle and Jill a ride back to their hotel, where he was
also staying—which touched off a series of awkward moments. Fiddle and Jill told him that they had their own car
but nonetheless got up to leave. Once in the car, they then
told Sidey their car wouldn't start and they had to go back to
the house to call for help. At that moment, the clouds of confusion parted for Sidey. "Hugh, you stupid guy," he told himself.

———

Although my White House adventure began because I had asked to interview Jacqueline Kennedy, I never once met— or even saw—her during my time there. One reason for this was that her office was in the East Wing and I was in the West Wing, and the two sides of the White House, though not a hundred yards apart, were separate worlds, operating independently of each other. Never did I hear one of my colleagues in the press office say they were going over to the East Wing.

But the main reason I never saw or met her was that she spent most of the summer of 1962 away from the White House. After her state visit with the President to Mexico in June—where she charmed her hosts by giving a short speech in impeccable Spanish—she basically left Washington for an extended three-month holiday. In addition to Glen Ora, where she often retreated for long weekends with her children, she had rented a seven-bedroom home in Hyannis, not far from the Kennedy compound. From August 7 to August 30, she was away with Caroline in Italy, and upon her return, she headed straight to Hammersmith Farm, her childhood home in Newport, Rhode Island, remaining there with her children until early October. Only then did she return to the White House. Which explains why the President had so much time for me.

Like so many young women in America at the time, I admired Mrs. Kennedy's regal poise and sense of style. (So did my mother, who had met her in 1961 when Mrs. Kennedy hosted Miss Porter's alumnae at the White House. My mother kept the invitation and an engraved White House matchbook in her photo album.) By all accounts, she was a devoted mother and supportive wife, a woman—as would later become abundantly clear—of great strength and character. It shames me, then, to admit that I don't recall feeling any guilt about my role in her life. In my nineteen-year-old mind, I wasn't invading the Kennedys' marriage. I was merely occupying the President's time when his wife was away. Probably because she was away all summer, she didn't loom over our interactions. With few exceptions, the President never talked about her when he was with me—and he certainly never said anything unflattering or critical. As in so many other things, it pains me now to say I simply took my cues from the President. If he wasn't troubled about his wife, why should I be?

I realize how blithe that sounds, but it's the truth. As I said before, I never thought that maybe I wasn't the only "other woman" in the President's life. I simply declined to think about it.

It wasn't until much later, when the biographies started coming out, that the full extent of his philandering began to dawn on me. Only then did I hear about women such as Helen Chavchavadze, yet another young Farmington graduate, and Mary Pinchot Meyer, a worldly socialite and dazzling former reporter, who acquired almost iconic status among biographers, in large part because they were among the few of the President's women who could be identified by name. Unlike me, these women weren't invisible. They had been an integral part of the Kennedys' social life for years, meeting their children, toasting their successes, and attending intimate dinners hosted by Mrs. Kennedy in the 1950s when she was a senator's wife and in the 1960s when she was First Lady.

As I read about these women—and figured out that the President was carrying on with some of them at the same time he was seeing me—I began to appreciate two things about him.

The first was the great care the President took to shield his wife from his infidelities. I believe he placed her on a pedestal as the perfect partner to help him realize his ambitions. And he planted that pedestal in a private space where all his "other women," including me, would never be permitted to enter.

The second was that, at all times, he was protecting himself, too. How do you do that while raising children and being a husband and leading a party and running a country and traveling the world, pursuing a vision of democracy?

You build walls, you compartmentalize, you make sure that no one ever knows you completely.

Chapter Seven

The President was quite vain, particularly about his hair. During that summer, he would frequently summon me to the Oval Office and ask me to administer a hair treatment before one of his televised press conferences. The hair treatments were apparently a daily ritual that originated during the 1960 campaign. He insisted on using products only from Frances Fox, a company in upstate New York. He liked to lean back in his rocking chair and close his eyes while I massaged some tonic and an amber-colored ointment into his scalp. Then I would brush—never comb—it all into place. Sometimes a visitor would walk in while this was going on, and the President would signal for me to continue, and talk to his visitor as I worked away.

When I wasn't giving hair treatments, I was continuing to work in the press office, running errands, answering phones, stocking office supplies, clipping the wires, handing out press releases, and filing press photos. But as the summer wore on, I began feeling less connected to the work. I was spending more of my time thinking about my affair with the President, and being pulled deeper into his personal orbit.

Despite all the time we spent together and the increasing level of familiarity between us, I never rose above being the obedient partner in our relationship; the inherent imbalance of power between us was simply too great. In all our time together, it never once occurred to me to call him Jack. Even in our most intimate moments, I called him Mr. President. I still do today. It is a frame of mind, I suppose, that never fades. Considering the trappings of power that surrounded him even when he was not in the public eye—the valet, the cooks, the Secret Service agents, the staffers like Dave Powers who, though close friends, all addressed him as Mr. President—it's not as strange as it sounds. To do otherwise would have seemed inappropriate.

The weekends the President went to Hyannis that summer were hazy, empty, aimless days for me. My roommate was usually out of town on weekends, leaving me to my own devices. I spent my days doing laundry and window-shopping in Georgetown, and my nights reading in bed. I had no social life to speak of. Only once do I recall going out, to a cocktail party in Georgetown given by young Jay Rockefeller, the future governor and senator from West Virginia. It seemed like everyone there was right out of college, working at real jobs for people of consequence. I worked for people of consequence, too, I thought, but in an inconsequential capacity. The fact that I was romantically involved with the most consequential person in town didn't do me much good here; it wasn't exactly something I could talk about. So I nursed my drink, concluded that I was totally out of place, and went home early. I couldn't wait for Mondays to come.

On late summer weekday afternoons, the President often left the office a little early and took guests on cruises along the Potomac River on the presidential yacht *Sequoia*. The *Sequoia* was a beautiful ship, built in 1925, 104 feet long, with a large main salon and several decks where guests could sip cocktails while a soft breeze took the edge off Washington's oppressive heat. Dave Powers was often on board, as were Massachusetts Congressman Torbert "Torby" Macdonald, the President's roommate from Harvard, and Paul "Red" Fay, the undersecretary of the Navy and an old wartime friend of the President's. The atmosphere was like a polite fraternity social event. There were more men than women, and the women were not necessarily married to the men they boarded with. I was always introduced as "Mimi who works for Pierre in the press office."

One afternoon, I was introduced to a woman who immediately sensed that I wasn't there in a press role. She was not naïve. She worked for—and was rumored to be having an affair with—Florida senator George Smathers. As we sipped drinks on the upper deck, she took me aside.

"You are too young to be here," she said. "You're going to regret it. All of a sudden you'll turn around and you'll be twenty-five and you won't have a life."

I felt like I'd been punched in the gut. *How did she know?* I summoned up my best Farmington poise and said, "I have no idea what you're talking about."

But I was a heedless girl, blinded by the President's power and charisma, and fully committed to keeping our affair secret. How else would I respond but with feigned ignorance and denial? In a way, what I said to her was true. Although I meant it as a mind-your-own-business brush-off, I really did have no idea what she was talking about. I didn't appreciate that I was too young, that I was out of my depth, that the dazzle of an affair fades with time, that it's not healthy to be at the perpetual beck and call of a married man, that there *would* be consequences to what I was doing. I wasn't even capable of imagining life at twenty-five; I was nineteen and having fun and living in the moment. Twenty-five seemed to be a million miles away.

In mid-August, the President and I were in the Oval Office, doing the hair treatment, when he asked me if I wanted to see Yosemite National Park. He said it with the casual air of someone asking if I wanted to go to the movies. He explained that his secretary of the interior, Stewart Udall, had been urging him to publicize the emerging issues of conservation and environmental protection, and a trip to several notable sites out west was now in the works. He said he thought I'd find it beautiful, and did I want to come?

The idea of such a trip, of course, was irresistible. I'd never seen Yosemite, and could count the number of times I'd been on an airplane on one hand. Yes, I said. I would love to go. The President said that Dave Powers would be making all the arrangements.

On Friday, August 17, the President embarked on the kind of whirlwind tour that only heads of state with advance teams and their own air force can achieve. First he stopped in Pierre, South Dakota, to dedicate the Oahe Reservation dam. Later that day, he was off to Pueblo, Colorado, to look at another water project, and receive a cast-iron frying pan—a symbol of the Old West—from a local pol. From there, he flew to California to spend the night in Yosemite National Park, and after that made a quick visit to the San Luis dam project in Los Banos, California.

I would be flying in the Air Force support plane, along with the luggage, press office equipment, and other White

House staffers. I was instantly seduced by the sultanic style of presidential travel. There was nothing left to chance, nothing to worry about. I was told where to drop off my suitcase at the White House and what car I was to ride in to Andrews Air Force Base. (The President wouldn't be with us; he flew by helicopter.) There was no fussing with tickets, no lugging of bags. My name was printed along with everyone else's name on the official passenger list—and if that caused resentment among other women in the press office who saw the list, I was oblivious to it. We were driven by motorcade past a military honor guard, out to Andrews Air Force Base. We were dropped off on the tarmac and climbed the long flight of stairs onto the plane, where we were greeted with platters of food and drinks. Upon arrival, we were told, our suitcases would be delivered directly to our rooms.

Yosemite was beautiful, a moonscape, unlike anything I'd seen before on the East Coast, but a pattern started there that, unfortunately, I would soon become accustomed to. I came to think of it as the Waiting Game. I sat around, waiting until the President needed me. That was my role. So while everyone in the President's retinue was free to wander the Ahwahnee Hotel—a hulking mountain lodge with massive stone fireplaces and painted wood-beamed ceilings situated within sight of Yosemite Falls—I never even left my room.

"Stay put," Dave had told me when we arrived. "I'll call you when the President wants you."

So that's what I did: I stayed put. I sat in a chair and stared out the window, watching an 1,100-foot ribbon of water cascade down a sheer granite cliff less than a mile away. Then as evening fell and daylight faded, I ordered room service and sat alone picking at my food, waiting for the President to call. In describing it now, it sounds as if I'm painting a melancholy scene. But if I harbored any thoughts of self-pity or loneliness in my room, I don't recall them. The truth is, I was thrilled to be part of the presidential entourage, thrilled to be getting out of stifling Washington, D.C., in the middle of August, and, most important, thrilled to be spending time with President Kennedy. I had been assigned a room three doors down from his suite. This would be the first night we'd ever spent together outside of the White House.

Around eight-thirty that night, Dave Powers appeared, and escorted me to the President's room. I knocked on the door, and the President answered. When I walked in, there was no hug or kiss. In fact, I don't remember the President *ever* kissing me—not hello, not goodbye, not even during sex. Instead, he greeted me with a cheery hello, seeming almost surprised that I was at the door. Then he relaxed in a chair, complimented me on how I looked, and asked about my day. I said nothing about how I'd spent the day in my room, waiting. Eventually he moved to sit on the edge of the bed, and took off his shoes. He needed help with his shirt to protect his back and, by this point in our relationship, was fully aware that I would come over to help without his having to ask. And I did.

I can't say our relationship was romantic. It was sexual, it was intimate, it was passionate. But there was always a layer of reserve between us, which may explain why we never once kissed. The wide gulf between us—the age, the power, the experience—guaranteed that our affair wouldn't evolve into anything more serious. Nor did I harbor illusions that it would.

I knew my role and played it well. I was good company to him, in part because he hated to be alone but also because he found a change of pace in someone like me—young, full of energy, willing to play along with whatever he wanted. We joked about members of the press office staff and who was saying what about whom in the press corps. The President loved gossip, the juicier the better. He also loved to laugh. One day he surprised me by asking if I knew any school songs from my days at Miss Porter's. It was an odd request, but I obliged. As I began to sing one, he started chuckling. It wasn't the response I was going for, but I understood why. Beyond my froggy singing voice, he just couldn't resist a girl with a little bit of Social Register in her background.

Friends never hesitate to ask if I was in love with President Kennedy. My guarded answer has always been "I don't think so." But the truth is, "Of course I was." This was one part hero worship, one part schoolgirl crush, one part the thrill of being so close to power—and it was a potent, heady mix. Then there was the spike in my self-esteem that I felt whenever I was with him; I simply felt more alive—more special—in his company. But I want to be clear: I knew the situation. I knew that ours wasn't a partnership of equals, and that my love would go unrequited. He was the leader of the free world, after all. The married leader of the free world. And I wasn't even old enough to vote.

After Yosemite, we flew to Los Angeles, and I was moved into the Beverly Hilton hotel in Beverly Hills. The President spent Saturday and Sunday afternoon with his sister Pat and brother-in-law Peter Lawford, at their beach house in Santa Monica while I remained at the hotel, playing the Waiting Game until he returned to see me in the evenings. This wasn't exactly a hardship. The hotel, with its gorgeous grounds and enormous swimming pool, had more than enough diversions to keep me occupied.

The return from California to Washington was the one and only time I flew on Air Force One. It was a fluke, really; a seat had opened up when a staffer returned to Washington early, and it was offered to me. As was the custom for all passengers on Air Force One, I boarded the plane well ahead of the President. I sat in the rear, just in front of the kitchen, along with other junior staffers. A conference room was between us and the President's section, where seating was reserved for the inner circle—in this case, Kenny O'Donnell, Dave Powers, Pierre Salinger, and Larry O'Brien, the President's liaison with Congress, as well as Secretary Udall. The seats were roomy and plush, and everything bore the presidential seal. It would have been normal for any first-time passenger to take a souvenir—a napkin, a coaster, a matchbook—but I didn't want to feel like an ordinary visitor, so I resisted.

I went on one other trip with the President that summer, to places a little less scenic than Yosemite and Beverly Hills. The space race with the Soviet Union was high on his agenda, and he was determined that the United States be the first country to land a man on the moon. So the itinerary included the nation's major air and space facilities: the National Aeronautics and Space Center in Huntsville, Alabama; Cape Canaveral in Florida; the new manned space flight center in Houston; and finally the McDonnell Aircraft Corporation in Saint Louis, where parts for NASA's Mercury and Gemini programs were made. This was a nonstop two-day tour with only one overnight in Houston. Once again I flew on the support plane, which was packed with VIPs: Vice President Lyndon Johnson was there, as were Cyrus Vance, the secretary of the Army, James Webb, the director of NASA, and somewhat incongruously, the radio and

TV personality Arthur Godfrey, who was a pilot and an ardent voice for the airline industry.

The trip was a blur of arrivals and departures. My most vivid memory was the appearance of Vice President Johnson at my seat on the Florida-to-Houston leg of the trip. Johnson, towering above me, politely introduced himself as I struggled, unsuccessfully, to free myself of my seat belt and stand up. When I told the President later that night at the hotel that I'd met his vice president, he seemed to lose his composure for a split second. "Stay away from him," he said. At the time I found his response odd, but I realize now that he might have been alarmed that I had slipped out of the private compartment he had put me in. He might have worried that a politician as savvy as Lyndon Johnson—a living testament to the maxim "Knowledge is power"—could figure out who I was and why I was aboard and possibly use it to his advantage.

As the time approached for me to go back to Wheaton for my sophomore year, I pleaded with my parents to let me drop out and stay in Washington. They didn't seem concerned that I was willing to abandon my education for a lowly job—that is, if I could get one when my internship was up—at the White House. I wouldn't be the first person to be seduced by proximity to power or the glamour of the Kennedy Administration. Kennedy insiders called it "White House Fever," and as far as I could tell, everyone who worked there was afflicted with it. My parents assumed I had fallen in love with politics and that I was pursuing my true calling; they certainly didn't suspect that I had other, far more personal, reasons for staying in Washington. Ultimately, though, they vetoed my plan for financial reasons: They'd already paid my tuition for the year, and they weren't willing to throw that money away.

I understood, but I wasn't happy. I had experienced a liberating, exhilarating summer, and the thought of going back to Wheaton, a quiet all-girls college with strict rules, was depressing.

When I told the President about my plans, he promised to call me often when I was back at school. When I pointed out that such a call might create problems for him, he said he had already considered that. He would use the pseudonym Michael Carter. He teased me that my return to college was more like abandonment—of him. Then he would cue up Nat King Cole's version of "Autumn Leaves" on the stereo in the residence, making me pay close attention when the lyrics came to, "*But I miss you most of all, my darling, when autumn leaves start to fall.*" He had a mushy sentimental streak and wasn't afraid to show it.

Just before I left, I bought him another copy of that record. I trimmed the cover with leaves I'd collected in a park, and gave it to him as a farewell present.

"You're trying to make me cry," he said.

"I'm not trying to make you cry, Mr. President," I said. "I'm trying to make sure you remember me."

Chapter Eight

To my surprise, the President *did* remember me.

In mid-September 1962, I was firmly back in school, having moved into the sophomore dormitory at Wheaton, and started classes. Within a week I received my first phone call from Michael Carter.

Even with all the meetings and public appearances in his day, President Kennedy was known to average fifty telephone calls a day, many before he left the residence in the morning or when he returned in the evening. The phone, he told me, was his lifeline to the everyday world. When we were together at the White House, he was always calling friends, members of Congress, his brothers and sisters. He was incapable of sitting still, or of not using a moment of free time to scavenge for information or a good laugh, some form of human connection.

He called me in the evening when he knew I would be in my room and, presumably, when he was alone. There were no phones in our dorm rooms, however; we received calls on a house phone in a closet on the first floor. The President would call that number. Sometimes the girl on phone duty would yell the caller's name. The President's Boston pronunciation of "Carter" sounded more like "Cotta" and that's the name that would be broadcast down the hall: "Mimi Beardsley, Michael Cotta for you."

Amazingly, no one ever recognized his voice. When I came on the line, he always seemed completely unworried about being identified. He had a keen sense of what he could risk, how far he could push his behavior, and at what point he would be legitimately vulnerable or exposed. His survival instincts must have told him that no young women would suspect that a man named "Michael Carter" on a dormitory phone could possibly be the President of the United States.

The President would pepper me with a million little questions over the phone, as if he had all the time in the world: What were the courses I was taking? Were the teachers good? What was I reading? Were the girls interesting? What did they talk about? What did I have for dinner? It was so like him. In temperament, he was an inexhaustibly, relentlessly curious man. He would poke and prod anyone—from cabinet members to assistants—who could supply him with fresh information, a bit of news.

Evidently, that insatiable curiosity extended to the sophomore class at Wheaton. My stories about college life seemed to amuse him; he always listened patiently, was never curt with me, never sounded unengaged. He acted like he had all the time in the world for my stories. When he asked specifically about *my* social life, I resisted the urge to sound more interesting and make up dates with young men that never happened. The truth was I still didn't have a social life— a couple of blind dates here and there but nothing that made a lasting impression. What college sophomore could stand a chance against the President?

Perhaps he enjoyed talking to me precisely because I was so young and naïve. We didn't talk politics or national security or the news of the day. I didn't bother him with questions about life in the White House or his plans for the weekend. I simply talked about my life and its simple day-to-day dilemmas—dealing with a difficult dorm mate or a dull teacher—and he seemed to find some relief in this.

"When can you come to Washington?" the President inevitably asked at the end of each conversation. I would pull out my calendar, and we would make a date.

From there, Dave Powers would handle all the arrangements. A car service would pick me up at my dorm and drive me three hours to LaGuardia airport in New York. On the way down, I would catch up on some school reading and stop at a beauty parlor in Rhode Island to have my hair washed and combed out while the car waited. When I arrived at LaGuardia, there would be a prepaid ticket waiting for me at the Eastern Airlines shuttle desk, and after landing at National (now Reagan) Airport in Washington, I would be greeted by a driver holding a sign reading "Michael Carter." Off we'd go to the White House.

I think of this image often, fifty years later: me in the backseat of a black limousine in 1962, catching up on homework, shutting out the fact that I was nineteen and on my way to the nation's capital for the purpose of hopping into bed with the President. That kind of duality was so like me then: the obedient daughter running through her checklist of things to do, no matter what else was happening around her. I guess I knew a little bit about compartmentalizing, too.

Only when I was in the limousine, on the way to the White House, did my thoughts turn to the President. I'd check my hair and face in the compact mirror in my purse, although I still didn't wear any makeup or lipstick. I'd rehearse an item or two that I wanted to share with the President. The "White House Fever" that had made me want to abandon college for a job in Washington had not dissipated; it was simply hidden away, a big secret that I couldn't share with anyone at Wheaton. I kept myself busy maintaining a B-plus average. I was either in class, in the library, or in the dorm. But as I was on the bridge crossing the Potomac River from Virginia to the District of Columbia and the White House came into view, those old feelings would come back to me powerfully. It was then that I realized how much I missed the people at the White House, and the vitality I felt there.

Oddly, my trips to Washington never raised any suspicion among my friends at school. The college insisted that all girls sign out in a log book at the front door of the dorm whenever we left campus, indicating where we were going, where we were staying, and when we planned to return. My teachers and the dean of students were so impressed by the White House as my destination that they never questioned where I was going to stay. If anyone asked, I'd tell them I was staying "with a girlfriend in Georgetown," adding that the White House press office always needed extra help on the weekends. While the part about the White House needing help may have been technically accurate, it wasn't true for me. I rarely visited the press office on my trips there. I spent my time in the residence.

On my second "date" trip to Washington, in October 1962, I was greeted on Saturday afternoon by a President who was not his usual ebullient self. He was tense and quiet and preoccupied, with dark bags under his eyes—and for the first half-hour together I wondered why I'd been asked to come down to be with him. That night, he was distracted and on the phone constantly.

He had a lot on his mind. A few days earlier, on October 1, after a series of legal challenges that ended in the U.S. Supreme Court, James Meredith had become the first black student to be admitted to the University of Mississippi. When Meredith showed up for class, however, he was physically barred from entering the university by the state's governor and lieutenant governor, forcing President Kennedy to take legal action against the governor and send military personnel to the university to protect Meredith. Riots followed in which two people died, but in the end Meredith took his first class at Ole Miss and the President had demonstrated his resolve on a major social issue that he had been avoiding since his inauguration. As a result, his approval ratings had shot way up. By all rights, he should have been a happy man when I arrived.

But what I didn't know at the time was that the President was in the middle of what would become the most dramatic and tense episode of his presidency: the Cuban Missile Crisis.

When I left him that Sunday, I didn't hear from him for the next two weeks, which was highly unusual. I wasn't aware, of course, that during this time the President had authorized U-2 spy planes to fly over Cuba, revealing that the Soviets were secretly building bases for nuclear missiles only ninety miles from the U.S. mainland. But by October 22, the news had broken, and I finally understood. It was a Monday morning in my comparative government class when Professor Minton F. Goldman interrupted his lecture to open a discussion about the President's scheduled speech to the nation that night at seven o'clock. We all knew he would address the conflict with the Soviet Union over missiles in Cuba. I desperately wanted to be in Washington with him, but like everyone else, I would have to make do with watching on television.

My dorm didn't have a television set, so I went over to the Student Alumnae Building, and there, on the black-and-white TV, was the President, looking more serious than I had ever seen him. The fear in the room was palpable. Some of the girls were holding hands. I stood in the back with my arms crossed. It's hard to convey the tension in the air as the President articulated the dire situation we found ourselves in, and explained the unprecedented threat to the nation. When he reminded us that "the greatest danger of all would be to do nothing," I looked around the room and realized that none of the other girls was thinking what I was thinking.

As I walked back to the dorm, I remember feeling not fear but urgency. Although I had become adept at compartmentalizing my secret White House life when I was at Wheaton, this was different. I suddenly wanted to be in Washington. I wanted to be in the press office. I wanted to be in the middle of all that energy and purpose. I wanted to be part of things. This may have been the first time I thought of President Kennedy in historical rather than personal terms. In this moment, he wasn't my lover, he was the man with the nation's security in his hands.

That night, I called the White House, and the switchboard operators, who knew me well by that point, put me through to Dave Powers.

He was clearly under enormous stress and didn't have time to talk. "None of us knows what's going to happen, Mimi," he said curtly. "I'll get back to you closer to the weekend."

The next four days passed in slow motion. The Cuban Missile Crisis, as it became known, was all over the news, creating an atmosphere of deep concern in some quarters, and outright hysteria in others. We were warned about a national shortage of bomb shelters. We were besieged with apocalyptic estimates about how many people would die in a nuclear exchange between the Soviet Union and the United States. I must admit that I felt a sense of dread, if not panic, myself—and my admittedly naïve response was the belief that if I could only get to Washington, all would be well. It didn't make any rational sense, but I felt if I could be close to the President and in the building where the decisions were being made, then somehow I would feel safer, more secure.

The following Friday, Dave Powers called my dorm. I ran to the phone. "Come to Washington," he said. "Mrs. Kennedy is going to Glen Ora. I'll send a car."

I packed my overnight bag and signed out the next morning.

When I pulled up to the South Portico at the White House, I went directly upstairs as usual. There Dave and I played the Waiting Game in the residence living room, the one next to the President's bedroom, while the President remained in a meeting downstairs with a group of close advisers known as EX COMM, the Executive Committee of the National Security Council. They had convened at the White House to deal specifically with the Cuban crisis. The President joined us after a while, but his mind was clearly elsewhere. His expression was grave. Normally, he would have put his presidential duties behind him, had a drink, and done his best to light up the room and put everyone at ease. But not on this night. Even his quips had a halfhearted, funereal tone. At one point, after leaving the room to take another urgent phone call, he came back shaking his head and said to me, "I'd rather my children be red than dead." It wasn't a political statement or an attempt at levity. These were the words of a father who adored his children and couldn't bear them being hurt.

Later in the evening, he urged Dave and me to eat the now-cold supper of roast chicken that had been prepared for us. As we began serving ourselves, Bobby Kennedy called to say he was on his way over. When he arrived, I withdrew to the bedroom so he wouldn't see me. As a result, I wasn't a firsthand witness to the exchange between Dave and the President, as reported in Richard Reeves's 1993 biography, *President Kennedy: Profile of Power,* which perfectly encapsulates Dave's role as First Friend. Evidently, as they talked, Bobby was painting a gloomy, end-times picture of the crisis, while Dave just kept on eating.

"God, Dave," the President said, "the way you're eating up all that chicken and drinking up all my wine, anybody would think it was your last meal."

"The way Bobby's been talking, I thought it was my last meal," Dave said.

When the President and his brother went back downstairs to yet another EX COMM meeting, Dave filled me in on what was going on. The President was confident—much more than Bobby—that the crisis could be peacefully resolved. He had just sent a letter to Khrushchev offering an end to the naval quarantine and a promise not to invade Cuba if Khrushchev removed the missiles. Now he was waiting, along with the rest of the world, for the Soviet premier's reply.

That I was present at all in the residence on that evening strikes me now as surreal. God knows I didn't belong there. But it was intoxicating. At that moment, I would rather have been there than anywhere else on earth.

But the Cuban Missile Crisis taxed the poise of even the Great Compartmentalizer. Although our get-togethers were always quite sexually charged, it wasn't to be on this occasion. Dave and I waited up a while longer for the President, but his meeting dragged on past eleven o'clock, so I decided to go to bed. I was asleep by the time he finally came upstairs again. He unwound that night by watching *Roman Holiday* with Dave.

The next morning I got up early, needing to head back to school. The President was already awake, sitting in bed and working the phones as I waved goodbye just before eight A.M. Thus, he was alone that Sunday morning, October 28, when word came that there would be an important announcement from Moscow at nine A.M. I was sitting on a train, somewhere between Washington and Providence, when President Kennedy was told that the Soviets had accepted his terms and agreed to remove their missiles from Cuba. Like everyone else in America, he heard it via a radio announcer in Moscow reading Khrushchev's letter.

The relief in the White House must have been extraordinary. This was as close to the brink of "mutually assured destruction" as we had ever come. Many of the President's advisers, I would read later in Pierre Salinger's memoir, had slept in their offices, including members of the press office. Pierre himself had moved into a hotel one block from the White House so he could rotate night duty with his deputy press secretaries. Barbara Gamarekian recalled in a 2001 *New York Times* column that she'd been assigned the first night shift and had slept in a bomb shelter in the basement. What really "got my attention," she wrote, was being handed a card in a white envelope telling her to report to the North Portico in the event of an evacuation. When she went home the next morning to change clothes, one of her housemates was getting in a car and driving to Florida, trying to escape Washington. The nation's capital was in terror.

I don't remember it that way. Here's how I remember it: As President Kennedy met with the men he had chosen to handle the crisis, including "best and brightest" figures such as Defense Secretary Robert McNamara and National Security Adviser McGeorge Bundy, I was sleeping like a baby, wrapped in soft linens, in a bedroom on the second floor of the White House. At that moment, it felt like the safest place I could be.

Chapter Nine

Even in a college dormitory full of nineteen-year-old women, I can't remember ever talking to my classmates about sex, let alone sex with the President. Sex was a closed subject back then: There was no nudity in movies, television was chaste and wholesome; advertising was corny and square by today's coarse standards. Yes, Helen Gurley Brown's groundbreaking *Sex and the Single Girl* had been published in 1962—and reportedly sold two million copies in its first three weeks of publication—but the subject of sex was still treated with so much modesty that her chapter on contraception was removed from her book before publication. Not only that, she was often barred from repeating the word *sex* in her television appearances. I never read the book, anyway. Nor did I read the racy novels of the time, such as Grace Metalious's *Peyton Place* or Rona Jaffe's *The Best of Everything*. These were popular novels back then precisely *because* they dealt with sex. But among my crowd, boy crazy as some of us were, the topic of sex was taboo. There was something of a cult back then about maintaining our virginity as long as possible, hopefully until our wedding night.

I hadn't even had the Conversation with my mother or older sister. My family, it's strange to recall now, wasn't paying that much attention to me. They thought of me as a well-behaved young woman who had a coveted summer job at the White House and spent the rest of the year studying at college. I also didn't have the kind of open relationship with my mother in which she expected me to tell her everything, or in which I could go to her with intimate problems or questions. There was so much that went unsaid. She still had a teenage boy and girl at home to raise, plus a busy homemaking and social life. It wasn't that she willfully ignored me; she simply didn't worry about me. She figured I could take care of myself.

If I had wanted to tell anyone, it probably would have been my sister Buffy, who was four years older and working in Philadelphia at the time. I suppose I could have told her immediately after that first encounter with President Kennedy. It would have been an uncomfortable conversation, but I could have broached the subject with her, maybe highlighting that I had lost my virginity but not revealing to whom specifically. But that was a Pandora's box, one I sensed that, once opened, could never be shut. If I'd told her, she would have hounded me until I told her whom I had slept with, and then she would have felt compelled to act on that information, which meant she very likely would have told my parents, who would have demanded that I end my internship at White House. And I didn't want that.

So I chose to lock it away and not say a word about it.

This is how a secret begins.

If the President had been nothing more than a summer fling, keeping my secret among my Wheaton classmates would have been relatively easy. But this wasn't a fling. The relationship continued into the fall and winter, requiring many trips to see the President, which made me self-conscious about any mention of him. I was worried about being in a situation where I might let something slip, so I responded by retreating into myself and becoming a bit of a loner. I didn't participate in college events or make many friends. I didn't hang around in the "smoker"—the smoking room in the dorm basement—where girls would relax over cigarettes and gossip. I almost never talked about my life. What could I say that wouldn't feel like a lie? The safest course, I decided, was to remain silent.

Because my overriding goal was to protect the President's and my reputations, I withdrew even from my roommates, who had also been classmates at Farmington. I doubt they noticed any drastic change in my personality; I didn't stay in bed all day or pout or sigh dramatically at odd moments. I wasn't terribly distracted in that lovesick way. I was just withdrawn and on guard, and it was a stance that clouded my relationships with friends for years.

My relationship with the President, however, maintained its intensity through the winter as he continued to beckon me to the White House and request my presence on presidential trips. Not all of these trips were unqualified delights. One, in particular, sticks out in my mind for its wonderful highs and its devastating lows.

In early December, the President was scheduled to go on a tour of eleven western states. Dave Powers called me to see if I could meet up with the entourage in Albuquerque, New Mexico, at the tail end of the trip. After that, we would go on to Bing Crosby's house in Palm Springs for some much-needed R&R. Yet again, I would have to sign out from Wheaton and travel to Washington to catch the backup to Air

Force One—with one crucial difference: I was no longer part of the press office. I was on board an official White House plane as a civilian, which, according to oral histories at the Kennedy Library, made at least one unnamed reporter curious about my role. (And, in retrospect, for very good reason: a college sophomore on the President's plane?) Pierre Salinger, who was as skilled as anyone in the world at deflecting reporters' suspicions, must have smoothed over any concerns, because nothing ever came of it.

When we got to Albuquerque, I joined Fiddle on a magnificent horseback ride through the high desert. We rode until sunset, after which I returned to the hotel to wait for the President and Dave Powers, and then proceeded to regale them with vivid descriptions of my afternoon as we dined in the President's suite. It had been a wonderful day, and the President seemed genuinely happy.

The next day, we headed out to Bing Crosby's house in Palm Springs, where a large festive crowd—many from the entertainment industry—had gathered to greet President Kennedy. I felt like I'd been admitted into some wonderful, secret club.

But then the evening turned into a nightmare.

I'd seen flashes of the President's darker side, which emerged rarely and only when we were among men he knew. That's when he felt a need to display his power over me. Although my admiration for him remains steadfast to this day, it is the darker aspect of his nature that I find hard to reconcile with all his admirable qualities. In revealing this side of his personality now, I realize yet another damaging note will be added to the record, but I cannot airbrush or ignore his actions during his darker moments; they remain a stain on my memory.

Crosby's house was a modern, sprawling single-story ranch in the desert, and the party was raucous. Compared to what I'd seen in Washington, this was another planet. There was a large group of people, a fast Hollywood crowd, hovering around the President, who was, as always, the center of attention. I was sitting next to him in the living room when a handful of yellow capsules — most likely amyl nitrite, commonly known then as poppers — was offered up by one of the guests. The President asked me if I wanted to try the drug, which stimulated the heart but also purportedly enhanced sex. I said no, but he just went ahead and popped the capsule and held it under my nose. (The President, with all his ailments, was accustomed to taking many medications and was reported to rely on amphetamines for energy. But he didn't use the drug himself that evening: I was the guinea pig.) Within minutes of inhaling the powder, my heart started racing and my hands began to tremble. This was a new sensation, and it frightened me. I panicked and ran crying from the room, praying that it would end soon, that I wasn't about to have a heart attack. Dave Powers, bless him, ran after me and escorted me to a quiet corner in the back of the house, where he sat with me for more than an hour until the effects of the drug wore off.

I didn't spend that night with President Kennedy. He was staying in a suite, now known as the Kennedy Wing, with its own private entrance on one side of the Crosby property. Was he alone? I do not know. For the first and only time since I met him, I was relieved not to see him — and fell asleep in one of the guest rooms.

This wasn't my first dark moment with the President, however. He had been guilty of an even more callous and unforgivable episode at the White House pool during one of our noonday swims at the end of the summer. Dave Powers was sitting poolside while the President and I swam lazy circles around each other, splashing playfully. Dave had removed his jacket and loosened his tie in the warm air of the pool, but he was otherwise fully clothed. He was sitting on a towel, with his pants legs rolled up, and his bare feet dangling in the water.

The President swam over and whispered in my ear. "Mr. Powers looks a little tense," he said. "Would you take care of it?"

It was a dare, but I knew exactly what he meant. This was a challenge to give Dave Powers oral sex. I don't think the President thought I'd do it, but I'm ashamed to say that I did. It was a pathetic, sordid scene, and is very hard for me to think about today. Dave was jolly and obedient as I stood in the shallow end of the pool and performed my duties. The President silently watched.

Much as I try, I cannot bring back anything—any emotion or thought—from that episode that would begin to explain why, without hesitation, I obeyed the President's command. Perhaps I was carried away by the spirit of playfulness I felt around him. Perhaps I was in thrall to his charm and authority. No doubt some of this had to do with my own insecurity and my need for his approval. A part of it also has to be that the three of us felt close to one another—in the way that co-conspirators feel connected to the people they're conspiring with. Dave Powers and I were umbilically linked to each other in our devotion to President Kennedy, and in the illicit relationship that Dave had played an essential role in fostering. And now the man who engaged our complete loyalty had gone too far. He had emotionally abused me and debased Dave. For what? To watch me perform for him and to show Dave how much he controlled us?

I was deeply embarrassed afterward, and I climbed out of the pool and went to the dressing room. I could hear Dave speak in as stern a tone as I ever heard him use with his boss.

"You shouldn't have made her do that," Dave said.

"I know, I know," I heard the President say.

Later, a chastened President Kennedy apologized to us both.

I have a deep well of affection for Dave Powers, who died in 1998 at age eighty-five after spending three decades as museum curator of the Kennedy Library in Boston. He was one of the most entertaining men I've ever met, and he was nobody's fool. He deftly blended his jovial personality with a serious, win-at-all-costs commitment to President Kennedy. Richard W. Stevenson, who wrote Dave's obituary in *The New York Times,* captured him perfectly with this story.

> *Asked once about the most difficult moment he had faced in politics, he replied with a story about forgetting to bring black shoes to go with Kennedy's blue suit in the Democratic National Convention in 1952, forcing Kennedy to make a televised speech in brown shoes.*
>
> *"And after it was over," Mr. Powers said later, "to help him relax, I said, 'Mr. Senator, that was a brown shoe crowd if I ever saw one.'"*

That was the Dave Powers I knew, a man so devoted to JFK that he would be crestfallen when his boss had to wear brown shoes with a blue suit for a black-and-white telecast—but then could save the day, and his dignity, with a witty one-liner. But I also feel sympathy for Dave. I can only imagine some of the distasteful duties he had to carry out at the President's behest—because I know what he had to do when those duties involved me.

One of the more unsettling assignments Dave performed on my behalf occurred a few weeks after I returned to Wheaton in the fall of 1962. I was becoming increasingly worried that I might be pregnant, and when "Michael Carter" called, I told him so. I was worried, I said. My period was two weeks late. The President took the news in stride, but he shouldn't have been surprised. I knew nothing about birth control, and he never used protection with me (either because of his Catholicism or recklessness, I could never be sure).

An hour later, Dave Powers called the dorm and put me in touch with a woman who had information about a doctor in Newark, New Jersey. Abortion was illegal then, but if you had cash and a connection to a sympathetic doctor, you could obtain one fairly easily. I called the woman, identified myself, and received the name and number of the doctor. Dave must have had someone—at least once removed from him—alert her to expect my call. Any link between President Kennedy and an abortion doctor would have been explosive. Even the docile White House press corps couldn't have averted their eyes from that story.

That was pure Dave Powers: He handled the problem immediately, and with brute practicality. There was no talk about what I wanted, or how I felt, or what the medical risks of an abortion might be. Which was just as well. Whenever I tried to sit down and take a deep breath and run through my options in my mind, my screen went blank. I didn't have the tools to face my situation rationally—and with no one else to talk to about it, I slipped into a state of high anxiety.

In the end, it was a false alarm. I never contacted the doctor in Newark. My period arrived a few days later, and I let the matter drop. Neither Dave nor the President ever brought it up again.

I hasten to add that for the vast majority of my time with President Kennedy, he was a sweet and thoughtful and generous man. He lifted my spirits whenever I was with him, and I'm fairly sure that nearly everyone in the White House felt the same way. However, he did have his demons, and given the few glimpses I had of his more sinister side, I shudder to think what other cleanup jobs Dave Powers was asked to do for his boss. Dave seemed like he was too nice a person to feel good about any of these assignments, but if he helped ease the President's mind, I suspect he didn't lose much sleep over his role. Where the President was involved, I don't believe Dave Powers's first impulse was to distinguish right from wrong.

A week before Christmas, I joined the President in the Bahamas, where he was meeting with Harold Macmillan, the British prime minister. This time I did not fly on Air Force One or on the White House backup plane. Someone in the press office, presumably Chris Camp, must have complained to Pierre Salinger or made him aware of the press interest in my presence on the official flights. Instead, I flew commercially on a prepaid ticket, which was just fine with me. It was December in Massachusetts, and I was looking forward to some sun at the Lyford Cay Club, where the President's entourage was staying.

Traveling without the official cover of the press office came with a slight complication. It meant that I had to remain invisible the whole time I was at Lyford Cay; no one could know I was there. That was fairly easy to do, as long as I was relaxing alone in my luxurious villa, or when Dave Powers would come by to drive me to the President's rented home in the evenings after his official duties had ended. Most of the White House people were staying in rooms at the clubhouse, so the back-and-forth between my quarters and the President's wasn't on anyone's radar.

But when it came time to leave for the airport on Friday, Dave Powers made an uncharacteristic tactical error. I would be riding to the airport in Dave's car and we would drive over to the President's house with the rest of the entourage. Then we'd follow in the motorcade to the airport. Dave, however, was still intent on keeping me invisible. He told me to sit up front—not only that but to crouch on the floor of the car so that no one would see me. He'd forgotten, however, that I am 5'9". I did my best to fit under the dashboard, but when the motorcade drew up in front of the President's villa to pick him up, I was spotted.

Here's how Sally Bedell Smith, relying on Barbara Gamarekian's oral history at the Kennedy Library, described the scene in her book, *Grace and Power:*

> *When Kennedy was leaving Nassau on Friday after-noon, Mimi Beardsley quite literally popped up again. "As the entourage of cars pulled up in front of the house to pick up the President," Barbara Gamarekian recalled, Pierre Salinger and his aide Chris Camp "saw the top of a little head over the door" and "thought there was a little child sitting in the front seat of the car. Chris said to Pierre, 'Who could that child be?' and they walked over and looked in the car, and here seated on the floor was Mimi! She was sitting on the floor of a car so she wouldn't be seen by anyone. She'd been [in Nassau], apparently, for several days. They took one look and sort of backed away and didn't say anything."*

Here's the thing: Everything in the above passage is, no doubt, true. I was there and can attest to its veracity. But I wasn't aware of any of it while I was hiding under the dashboard in the hot sun. I didn't hear people talking outside the window, didn't sense people craning their necks to take a peek at the top of my head. I simply obeyed Dave Powers. I crouched down and—as I so often did—waited.

Why Dave felt the need to hide me in the first place still puzzles me. The President was going on from Nassau to Palm Beach. If I was supposed to be kept a secret, then why was I on the passenger list of the backup plane to Florida, along with Dave Powers, Kenny O'Donnell, Llewellyn Thompson, the U.S. ambassador to the Soviet Union, and so many others? Why was I permitted to sit in the back of the plane, in full view of everyone, on the flight home?

I dwell on this incident because it highlights a couple of the tricks that memory plays on us.

For one thing, it showcases how people have different motives for not only what they remember but how they choose to share it. Barbara Gamarekian retold this story because it was a vivid "gotcha moment," one where she and others got ever so much closer to the "smoking gun" proof that the President was having an affair with me.

For me the incident highlights how keeping a secret colors—but doesn't wash away—our memory. It forces us to be selective, if only for self-preservation. If I hadn't read this paragraph about me in Bedell Smith's book, I don't think I would have recalled the crouching-in-the-car incident in quite this way—as a comical highlight of my trip that week. I'd recall how luxurious and decadent spending three full days in the Caribbean sun were compared to being holed up indoors in New England with my classmates. I'd recall how relaxed the President was and how unusual it was for me to spend three consecutive nights with him. I'd recall how my family commented on my tan when I returned home for Christmas. But as for ducking down in the car, I let that particular moment recede from my memory, as many of us would do when confronting a needless humiliation from our past. Only when I read about it did it come back to me.

I realize now that I suffered two humiliations that day. The first was in having to hide in the car. The second was that the people in the press office knew about me, were talking behind my back, and were laughing at me.

I wonder which is the greater humiliation, but I don't wonder why I kept my secret for so long. I wasn't keeping it only from everyone around me. I was also keeping parts of it from myself.

Chapter Ten

"I met someone," I told the President in the winter of 1963. I said it in a teasing way but also with a note of pride, as I rarely had anything substantive to report about my social life when he asked. And he always asked. "I went to Williams College on a blind date."

"Williams!" he exclaimed. "How could you?"

"Not everyone goes to Harvard, Mr. President."

During this particular conversation—the President had called me at Wheaton—he pressed me for details, but after just one date I was short on specifics. All I could say was that my date was "really nice."

The President continued to feign shock. "Ah, Mimi," he said, "you're not going to *leave* me, are you?"

"Of course not," I assured him, and it was true. The thought of extricating myself from the President had never occurred to me. But it would in time.

The young man in question was Tony Fahnestock, a senior at Williams. Only later would he tell me that his invitation to join him at the college's Winter Carnival had been a shameless ploy. He wasn't interested in me; he was keen on meeting my beautiful blonde classmates, Wendy Taylor and Kirk Dyett.

I'd seen Tony once before, from a distance, when I was sixteen and working as a mother's helper in the summer of 1959. We were at the Seabright Beach Club in New Jersey, and he was sitting with a group of eighteen-year-old boys and girls under a green-and-white striped umbrella while I was keeping my little charges from drowning in the baby pool. A two-year age difference is an enormous gap when you're a teenager. I remember watching Tony's group lounging about and laughing, envying their cool sophistication, and wondering if I could ever be like them. So I was surprised when he called me, out of the blue, at Wheaton; he wasn't someone I ever thought I'd run into again.

The first thing I noticed when he picked me up at the bus station in Pittsfield, Massachusetts, were his dark, crescent-shaped brown eyes. They gave him an endearing, sleepy look. He was two inches taller than I, which was a relief for someone my height. He wasn't brash and loud and overconfident, and he didn't talk about himself excessively. He was quiet and serious, and I liked that immediately.

Tony was busy taking special State Department exams for most of the weekend; he was considering joining the CIA. Our date was basically the Saturday-night dance, where I had to coax Tony out on the dance floor. We surprised each other by hitting it off from the beginning, to the point that Tony soon forgot all about my beautiful classmates and began to focus only on me. I knew that something special was happening when he insisted on driving me all the way back to Wheaton on Sunday, nearly a three-hour ride in weekend traffic, instead of sending me off at the Pittsfield bus station.

That was the sum total of my knowledge of Tony when I told President Kennedy that I had "met someone." Whether I was eager to have a serious boyfriend or sensed that Tony was "the one," I cannot say. What I could be sure of was that, on paper, Tony was a perfect match for me—and I for him. Our families were similar, well off, and members of the same kinds of clubs. Tony had gone to a good boarding school, Brooks, and had bright prospects for the future. I had been raised to be with someone like Tony.

In the following weeks, I visited Tony twice at Williams—and then he started coming to Wheaton to see me. It was a new feeling to have a boyfriend so devoted to me. It was heady and intoxicating, and also deeply confusing—because it made me confront my continuing, and one-sided, relationship with the President. Although Tony and I were not "going steady," as we used to say about a serious relationship, there was no doubt in my mind that he was my boyfriend, and a very desirable one. At some point, I knew, I would have to make a decision about the President. But I wasn't ready to do that yet.

As winter melted into spring, I began seeing Tony practically every weekend, either at Williams or at Wheaton. We didn't have an intimate relationship at this point. He never pressed me for sex.

While his gentlemanly behavior was quite attractive, this situation did pose a bit of a conundrum for me. I was physically attracted to Tony *and* I had learned the pleasures of sexual intimacy from President Kennedy. This created a yearning in me for something more than necking in dorms and cars. But pushing for sex with Tony would have raised questions; girls like me didn't do that back then. I might have to explain why it wasn't my first time, and that wasn't a conversation I wanted to have.

When I wasn't spending weekends with Tony, I was spending them with the President. Tony wasn't curious—or suspicious—about my other life in Washington. Why would he be? When we had started dating, I had already spent a full summer at the White House—and I had warned him that I continued to be needed by the press office even while I was at college. He not only accepted that lie, he was impressed by it. One time, after I told him I might be returning to the White House for a second summer internship, Tony proudly introduced me to his favorite professor at Williams, Frederick Rudolph. Dr. Rudolph, an eminent historian, was moving to Washington with his family that summer for a sabbatical year, and Tony wanted him to know that I would also be there, working in the White House.

Until then, I had never been a duplicitous person. I had lied only once that I can recall—to my mother, about an unattractive dress that she wanted me to take on a trip. I told her I'd taken it with me, but I'd really left it behind in my room. My lie was discovered when she found the dress. Beyond that, I considered myself a morally centered person, someone who knew right from wrong. Most of us think of ourselves that way, I suppose—that we're decent human beings. But I thought of my honesty as a defining aspect of my personality, a core value. I wasn't a saint, but if someone had asked me to identify my virtues as a person, I would have said that I was nice, that I wanted to be liked, that I was eager to please, and that I told the truth. It mattered to me that I had never knowingly hurt anyone by lying.

Now I was getting heavily involved with my first real boyfriend—and at the heart of the relationship was a massive, ongoing deception. A lie. Lying is inevitable when you're committed to keeping a secret. The lie becomes a sin of omission, not commission, but it's a lie nonetheless.

For the first time, it dawned on me that my secret life with the President might have consequences for someone other than me. Before I met Tony, my secret was my problem; it had no impact on anyone else I knew. If I kept it until the day I died, no one would be any worse off. But that was changing as Tony and I became more serious about each other; trust would become essential.

Soon I was thinking about Tony constantly. Mine was the schoolgirl daydreaming that any young woman with a new beau engages in, the delicious, guilty pleasure of "he loves me, he loves me not." I even practiced writing *Mrs. Anthony E. Fahnestock* and *Mimi Fahnestock* in the margins of my notebook. With Tony I began to think we had a future together. With the President I began to realize that my attachment, however strong, had no future; it was both real and unrealistic.

I cannot locate the exact time or place when I realized that Tony Fahnestock was the man I loved. I often wonder why. It's possible I once knew but have simply forgotten. But it's also possible that in holding back the full truth of who I was, I was also holding back myself, which shut me off from experiencing the thrill of falling in love. That's just one of many ways my secret has cost me. I wouldn't wish it on anyone.

And yet, being with the President and having his undivided attention was like taking this incredibly potent self-esteem

drug. And that's a hard habit to kick. Despite the humiliations and uncertainty, I remained enthralled by his charisma
and the glamour of traveling with his entourage. My college
life of dorm rooms, cafeteria dining, fraternity parties, homework, and moviegoing paled by comparison with Air Force
One, Caribbean resorts, the Secret Service, and limousines.

Simply put, I was leading two lives and enjoying both of
them.

In the middle of March 1963, I accompanied the President to South Florida. He was taking the weekend to relax at
the family estate in Palm Beach before going to Costa Rica to
meet with Central American leaders. It wasn't deemed appropriate for me to stay at the house, so Dave Powers booked
me a room at a pink motel on South Dixie Highway in West
Palm Beach, where I played the Waiting Game in the morn-
ings and then, in the afternoon, the President would send a
car for me and we'd enjoy a few hours relaxing by the pool
together. In the evening, the President and Dave would go
for a sail on the family yacht, the *Honey Fitz*, and I returned
to the motel. The next day we followed the same routine.

After the President left for Costa Rica, I stayed at the
motel for two more days before flying back to New York. It
was an enjoyable respite. Too enjoyable, it turned out. I lay
out in the sun too long one day and got a severe case of sun
poisoning. Feeling feverish and nauseated, I panicked. Not
knowing what to do, I tracked down Dave Powers in Costa
Rica and called for help. From there he placed a call to the
motel's front desk—which was less than thirty yards from my
room—and instructed them to watch out for me, while I ad-
hered to a regime of cool baths and lots of water. If I hadn't
gotten sun poisoning, it could have been a nice short break
from school in midwinter. But the blisters on my chest were

unbearable, preventing me from sleeping for more than an hour at a time. For years afterward, whenever I went out in the sun, my chest would burn and remind me of that time.

It puzzles me now that I wasn't peevish about having to shuttle between my spare motel room—where I spent most of my time that weekend, watching TV—and the sumptuous setting of the Kennedy estate, where it seemed like a party was always under way. I suppose I should have felt cheapened by the experience, as if I was a second-class citizen who had to be hidden away, out of sight. But I honestly don't recall feeling that way. I remember feeling happy to be there. Such was the depth of my intoxication with the President.

That intoxication continued even as my feelings for Tony were deepening. If I was confused by my attachment to two men, I was masking it well. That spring, I hatched a plan to drop out of Wheaton after my sophomore year, complete a second summer in the press office, and then stay on full-time in Washington, where surely some sort of exciting job awaited me. The President would be running for re-election in 1964, and I figured I could work on his campaign. Fiddle had done the same thing three years earlier. She had dropped out of college to work on the first Kennedy presidential campaign, and she was certainly thriving.

This time, my parents did not try to persuade me to finish college. It was not uncommon then for girls to go to a two-year junior college or to leave college before graduating to marry or go to work. Tony, too, endorsed the plan.

So bewitched was I by my life in the White House, I didn't want it to end.

Had I known, though, how much ill will I was generating among the women in Pierre Salinger's office, I might not have been so eager to return. When I read the oral histories of Chris Camp and Barbara Gamarekian at the Kennedy Library, the few paragraphs about me were truly upsetting. "Mimi had no skills. She couldn't type," Barbara Gamarekian recalled. "She could answer the phone and she could handle messages and things but she was not really a great asset to us."

Chris Camp was also harsh, describing me as a "presidential favorite" whose "abilities and skills and capacity to maintain a job in the press office were not immediately apparent to anyone who was associated with her. . . . She did what she could, but she was not a typist; she did not take shorthand; she was not skilled in clerical or stenographic work. In other words, she was filling a chair which could have been filled by somebody else who had the needed skills."

Chris, as far as I know, didn't dislike me personally; at least she referred to me as a "very pleasant girl." But she clearly resented me on professional grounds. Presidential plane rides were the ultimate merit badge in the press office, and, in her eyes, I had done nothing to earn them. Chris had worked hard for years—on the President's Senate staff—to get to her position and, quite rightly, resented the ease with which I had gained my seat on Air Force One. In her oral history, she claimed she'd told Pierre more than once to "take her off the press plane, take her off Air Force One . . . and don't put her in motorcades."

Barbara Gamarekian, on the other hand, obviously disliked me and was also annoyed by how easily I had leapfrogged the normal rotation of personnel on the coveted presidential trips. "Mimi, who obviously couldn't perform any function at all, made all the trips," she said.

Barbara was wrong. I didn't make "all the trips," and I

can't apologize now for having been there. My biggest disappointment, in fact, was missing out on the President's trip to
Europe in June 1963, when he made his iconic "*Ich bin ein
Berliner*" speech in front of the Berlin Wall and then continued on, triumphantly, to Ireland, England, and Italy. In her
oral history, Gamarekian insists that I behaved like a spoiled
child over being left behind for this trip—and that I called
the President in tears while he was in Ireland to complain
that Helen Ganss, the woman left in charge of the press office, wouldn't let me have that Friday off. The President had
been "furious" after my call, Barbara said, and told Dave
Powers that if "he were back in Washington, Helen Ganss
would be fired this very instant."

That call never happened. It was Helen Ganss, not I, who
placed a call to the President to give him some information,
and I let out a mock wail in the background because I wasn't
on the trip. That's what he reacted to, and it was in jest. Why
wasn't I on the trip? he wanted to know. Who had prevented
me from going? Helen diplomatically said she didn't know,
which the President accepted at face value. No one got
fired—and I didn't get the day off.

I recount this silly episode because Barbara's story is
now part of the public record and is already finding its way
into recent biographies of the President. But it's not true. I
may have been a naïve and sometimes foolish young woman,
but I would never have bothered the President with such a
petty personal complaint.

Gamarekian's bitterness may have been justified. When I
returned for my second summer at the White House, the
President evidently told Pierre that I should replace Barbara
as overseer of the photo sessions in the Oval Office, and
Pierre complied. There's no way that would have pleased her.

Access to the Oval Office was the Holy Grail in the West Wing, and "a little girl in the office," as she described me, had wrested it from her.

In the end, I don't—I can't—blame either Chris or Barbara for their severe opinions about me. That first trip to Yosemite—where I spent hours imprisoned in my room, waiting for the President to call for me—taught me that my primary job had changed from being part of Pierre Salinger's staff to being part of the President's personal retinue. I wasn't really helping out with press office duties. I was there for President Kennedy—and not there for Barbara, Chris, or anyone else.

In early June, just before moving down to Washington for the summer, I went with Tony's parents to his graduation from Williams. My attendance officially signaled that we were "serious." Shortly thereafter, Tony went into Army Reserve training at Fort Dix in New Jersey, while I had arranged to room with two close friends from Farmington, Marnie Stuart and Wendy Taylor, in a floor-through apartment on R Street in Georgetown. Marnie had landed a job at the Peace Corps headquarters through a family connection, while I helped Wendy secure a job in the White House gifts department. (I asked the President, who was always keen to help out Farmington girls, for an assist.)

Because of my new Oval Office photo duties, I saw the President practically every day he was in the White House that summer. But I didn't sleep over in the residence anywhere near as often as I had the year before, because Mrs. Kennedy was expecting another child at the end of August, and the President spent much more time with her and the children in Hyannis Port. I also started to branch out a bit socially, and Marnie, Wendy, and I spent a lot of time together. We even went swimming in the White House pool, which is when they met the President. Dave had invited us for a swim, and we were paddling around in borrowed swimsuits when the President arrived in his customary jacket and tie. In short order, he had changed into a bathing suit and was floating alongside Marnie and Wendy, asking about their summer jobs, whether they were enjoying Washington, where they were from, et cetera. I should have warned them that the President was likely to show up, but I wanted to surprise them. The bewilderment and excitement on their faces when he appeared was worth it. But even I was surprised when the President called for a box of animal pelts to be brought down to the pool. He was planning to give Mrs. Kennedy a fur throw for Christmas, he explained, and wanted the opinion of three fellow Farmington girls about which fur was the softest.

One of the few things I didn't do with Marnie and Wendy that summer—and I regret this terribly—was attend the massive civil rights rally at the Lincoln Memorial, where I would have heard Dr. Martin Luther King, Jr., deliver his "I Have a Dream" speech in person. I had planned to go, and told the President so. There might be violence, he told me, so I didn't go.

On Wednesday, August 7, Mrs. Kennedy went into labor on the Cape and gave birth, five and a half weeks prematurely, to a baby boy named Patrick Bouvier Kennedy. The baby had respiratory distress syndrome, not an uncommon occurrence in premature, underweight babies. Though Patrick was tended to by the best doctors, he lived only a day and a half.

I had never seen real grief in my relatively short life until I saw the President when he returned to the White House while Mrs. Kennedy recovered for a few more days in the hospital. He invited me upstairs, and we sat outside on the balcony in the soft summer evening air. There was a stack of condolence letters on the floor next to his chair, and he picked each one up and read it aloud to me. Some were from friends, others from strangers, but they were all heartfelt and deeply moving. Occasionally, tears rolling down his cheeks, he would write something on one of the letters, probably notes for a reply. But mostly he just read them and cried. I did too.

In late August Tony called me from Fort Meade and begged me to come see him because he didn't have weekend leave and missed me terribly. I explained that I was expected home in New Jersey to celebrate my mother's birthday, but he was adamant.

The fact that Tony was stationed at Fort Meade in Maryland, only an hour's drive from Washington, was a result of the one and only time I ever sought a favor for my personal benefit from the President. As Tony neared the end of basic training at Fort Dix, he learned he was being assigned for the next six months to Fort Polk in Louisiana. That meant we would never see each other, so I asked the President to do something about it. We were alone in the Oval Office. I was tearing up as I pleaded my case. By then I knew I was in love with Tony and that I wanted him to be closer to Washington—and me. At first, the President joked about how much pleasure he was taking in removing his competition from the scene. But seeing my tears and distress, he quickly changed course. He said he would talk to his Army military aide, Major General Chester Clifton, and in a few days, Tony was reassigned to Fort Meade in Maryland.

Now Tony was insisting that I come see him that weekend.

"I need to tell you something," he said.

He was so insistent that I became worried. Had he discovered my secret? Had he decided to break up with me? I made some excuse to my mother about working overtime at the White House that weekend and took a bus to Fort Meade. Tony had asked me to bring a picnic lunch, which helped ease my fears about his motivations. As we sat on his scratchy Army surplus blanket in a corner of the parade ground, I spooned out chicken salad and waited to hear what was on his mind.

He got straight to the point.

"I want to marry you," he said. "Will you marry me?"

I wasn't expecting a marriage proposal, but I needed only a second to process the question. "Yes!" I said. I practically leapt on top of him and kissed him as hard as I could.

There are many reasons people say yes to a marriage proposal. Love ought to be the first reason, and mine was. But so is the need for security and certainty. I had just turned twenty that May and felt, as young people do, that I was dealing with so many unknowns. Where would I be working after the summer? How would this end with the President? Where would I live after Marnie and Wendy went back to college? When would I ever find a "catch" like Tony again?

In marrying Tony, I was opting for security. And perhaps grasping for an escape route from my crazy double life. But I was also doing exactly what girls of my generation and social sphere had been brought up to do: Back then, when you went to boarding schools like Miss Porter's and colleges like Wheaton, it was inevitable that you'd get invited for weekends at Williams or Brown or Amherst, where you might meet a fine young man who prepped at Brooks or Groton or Andover. The rest was up to you. In marrying Tony I was, in a way, fulfilling my destiny.

That could explain why my parents took the news of my engagement with pleasure rather than shock and why they were not worried for a second that I might be too young for marriage. My mother, after all, had married my father when she was twenty-one. Funny enough, it was my friends Marnie, Wendy, and Kirk who were completely taken aback by the suddenness of my engagement. I could see it on their faces, but they were far too polite to say anything at the time. Only much later would they share what they were *really* thinking when I told them: *Who is this guy? You've only known him eight months! And now you're getting married?*

Tony gave me an extravagant engagement ring created from two oval sapphires that had been his grandfather's cuff links surrounded by diamonds from his grandfather's stick pin. The engagement announcement ran in *The New York Times* on September 8, 1963, and, along with the obligatory information about schools and lineage, made note of my job in the White House press office.

If the President had any misgivings about my engagement, he didn't let on. He gave me an engagement present—two gold-and-diamond pins shaped like sunbursts. I hid them away, never showing them to Tony or to any of my friends. Later that fall, however, I took them out to show the President what they looked like against a yellow sleeveless dress I had bought on sale in Georgetown. It was the only time I ever wore them.

The President also gave me a photograph of himself, the iconic color image of him at the helm of his sailboat, *Manitou*. At the White House, Fiddle had been a wizard at faking his signature on photo requests, but he signed this one himself in my presence.

"To Mimi," he wrote, "with warmest regards and deep appreciation." He was smiling when he gave it to me. "Only you and I know what that really means," he said.

Marnie and Wendy returned to college in September. I stayed on at the R Street apartment for another two months, to finish up my work at the press office and to try and finish up my relationship with the President. What I didn't realize at the time—and only came to appreciate as I wrote this book—was that I didn't need to finish up with the President. In his sly and graceful way, he was finishing up with me.

The President asked me to join him on the road two more times that fall. There was a grand tour of midwestern and western states, from Minnesota to Nevada, in late September, and there was a quick trip to New England, where he would be receiving an honorary degree at the University of Maine. On the heels of that second trip, I flew up from Washington on another Air Force support plane to meet him in Boston, where he was headlining a Democratic fund-raiser that Saturday night. I invited Wendy to come up from Wheaton and join me in the President's suite at the Sheraton Plaza Hotel before his speech.

After a typically full day that also included attending the Harvard–Columbia football game in Cambridge and visiting the grave site of his son at Brookline Cemetery, the President was relaxing on a sofa when I arrived at about six-thirty. He was fully dressed for the black-tie fund-raiser in an elegant tuxedo with pointed lapels. Ted Kennedy, then in his second year as a U.S. senator, was in the room as well, enduring some teasing from the President about his tuxedo's less-than-au-courant shawl collar.

My most vivid memory from that evening was a moment before Wendy arrived, when the President, once again, tried to show off his power over me in front of other men. I could see that mischievous look come into his eye, the one that appeared when he was about to challenge someone to do something they'd never dream of doing.

I braced myself.

"Mimi, why don't you take care of my baby brother," he said to me in front of Teddy. "He could stand a little relaxation." It was Dave Powers in the White House pool all over again.

This time I felt a flash of anger. And for the first time, I stood up to him. "You've got to be kidding," I said. "Absolutely not, Mr. President." He immediately dropped the subject.

For years, I have thought about my response as a kind of turning point in my life. I had been struggling, since my engagement, about how to end our affair, and here I was finally asserting myself, finally saying no. It felt good. For much of my life, I thought of this moment as the moment that our relationship truly began to wind down.

In hindsight, though, I've come to see that our relationship began winding down long before Boston—and it was President Kennedy who had taken the lead. In forcing myself to catalog the times and dates when we were together, I have come to realize that the President and I had stopped being sexual partners at the end of the summer that year. When I was on the five-day trip out west in September, I didn't spend the night with him. When I was in Boston in October, I slept in my own bed at the hotel.

It's easy to see how I could have missed this. For one thing, throughout the summer, I had seen the President practically every day. I took it for granted that I was in his life. It's a testament to how much more I valued being in his presence—being *around him* rather than *with him*—that it had escaped me that he no longer needed me for sex. The President was changing the relationship, and I wasn't seeing it.

The tragic death of his son in early August and my engagement to Tony three weeks later were crucial signposts. The former must have filled him not only with grief but with an aggrieved sense of responsibility to his wife and family. Even an irrepressible Don Juan like him might think it unseemly to continue his philandering ways when his family needed him so much. As for my engagement to Tony, it's conceivable that the President felt bad about continuing to sleep with me now that I was formally attached to another man. Whatever the reason, it's clear to me that he was obeying some private code that trumped his reckless desire for sex—at least with me.

For the rest of that summer I continued to see the President every day in the Oval Office and float in and out of his private orbit. I continued to swim in the pool with him. There was no change in our personal regard for each other, or in his warmth. But now that I realize that he had been shutting down our sexual relationship, I find it pleasing—and consoling—to see our seamless and unchanged contact as proof that I wasn't just a plaything to him, that he enjoyed my company, and that if he had lived longer I might have been someone he would want in his life, someone who could work for him after his presidency, someone he would regard in a small but meaningful way as a friend.

Perhaps I'm flattering myself.

The last time I saw President Kennedy was in New York City at the Carlyle hotel.

My wedding was scheduled for early January, and in late October, I moved home to New Jersey to deal with my bridal responsibilities: finalizing guest lists, sending out invitations, assembling my trousseau, registering for gifts, and selecting my bridesmaids' dresses.

I had been scheduled to take one last trip with the President before my wedding. I vacillated about going, unsure about how I could tell my parents that I had to leave for a few days when I had all this wedding business to attend to.

"Tell them the press office is begging you," Dave suggested. But I didn't need to. Dave called a few days later to say the plans had changed. I was no longer on that trip. Instead, Dave asked if I could be in New York on November 15, when the President would be in town to address the AFL-CIO convention at the Americana Hotel. "He is going to be at the Carlyle hotel," Dave said, "and he really wants to see you."

I scheduled a few wedding-related errands in the city on that day and went to the Carlyle at about one P.M. The Kennedy family owned a sprawling duplex penthouse on the two top floors of the hotel, one of the city's grandest. The penthouse was filled with sunlight and had glorious views of

Manhattan, which was a nice distraction for me because, once again, I was stuck in a hotel playing the Waiting Game. I was about to leave when he arrived and said he had a wedding present for me. He reached into his pocket and handed me three hundred dollars.

"Go shopping and buy yourself something fantastic," he said. "Then come back and show me."

Three hundred dollars was a lot of money back then. I felt vulnerable carrying that much cash as I walked down Madison Avenue and turned east at Sixtieth Street toward Bloomingdale's. I asked a salesperson to point me toward the most expensive clothes, which turned out to be on the third floor. Although I loved clothes shopping, I had never done it with the equivalent of a blank check. I'd never paid more than fifty dollars for anything in my life, but I felt obligated to spend every penny of the President's gift. I finally settled on a light gray wool suit with a black velvet collar, and a pencil skirt that stopped at my knees. It wasn't a very imaginative purchase, I admit.

The President seemed a bit disappointed when I wore the suit back to the Carlyle to show him. I think he wanted me to buy something more daring, not a tailored wool suit, not something that was the definition of conservative.

He took me in his arms for a long embrace and said, "I wish you were coming with me to Texas." And then he added, "I'll call you when I get back."

I was overcome with a sudden sadness. "Remember, Mr. President, I'm getting *married*," I said.

"I know that," he said, and shrugged. "But I'll call you anyway."

Then I said goodbye, hopped in a cab, and took the train home to New Jersey.

I was hoping that the President was coming around to the fact that our relationship was shifting to new terrain because of my marriage. I'd determined to tell him in Texas that this trip with him would be my last. On the other hand, I was a little disappointed that I'd been dropped from the roster. But I understood why: Mrs. Kennedy had decided to go to Dallas with her husband.

Chapter Eleven

Tony's twenty-third birthday fell on Wednesday, November 20, so he drove up from Fort Meade in his blue Volkswagen Beetle to meet me at my parents' house. That night, we celebrated over a birthday cake and spent the next day fine-tuning the Beardsley guest list for the wedding. On Friday, we drove into Manhattan to pick up some dresses. We planned to continue on to his parents' house in Southport, Connecticut, to spend the night and finalize the Fahnestock invitations.

On our way out of Manhattan, bound for Connecticut, we stopped for gas on York Avenue and Sixty-first Street, just off the entrance to the FDR Drive. When I returned from the ladies' room, Tony was in the driver's seat, his head inclined at an odd angle toward the car radio, as if he needed to soak in every word the announcer was saying. He turned to me with a terrible, wide-eyed look I'd never seen before.

"President Kennedy's been shot," he said.

We sat in the car as we absorbed the news over the radio. There wasn't much to report yet. The President was alive and had been rushed to Parkland Memorial Hospital in Dallas. His condition was unknown. There were other casualties.

Then, more ominously, there was a report from UPI that the President's wounds "could be fatal." I knew UPI meant Merriman Smith, a respected White House correspondent whom I had seen often in the press office.* His voice prompted thoughts of Pierre and Fiddle. Where were they? Was Dave Powers all right? Where was Chris Camp? (I learned later she was in Dallas on Air Force One, typing a speech for the President to give that night in Austin.) In the moment, concentrating on members of the staff was so much easier than trying to comprehend what had happened to the President.

Through the windshield I could see other people on the street who were just learning the news. They moved slowly, as if in a trance, many with their hands over their mouths to stifle sobs.

I felt trapped in the car. I was itching to jump out, but where would I go? I said to Tony, who was still staring at the radio dial, "We should get going." I needed to move, to be distracted.

Tony drove north on the FDR Drive toward Connecticut. We said nothing, letting the radio fill in the silence. Three shots had been fired. Texas governor John Connally, who had been riding in the car with the President, was also wounded. The police were looking for a white man wearing a white shirt and Levi's whose rifle had been spotted in a window of the nearby Texas School Book Depository.

Then, at two o'clock P.M., another bulletin, this one official: The President was dead.

I didn't believe it at first. The news was too sudden, too soon after the hopeful bulletin that he had been shot but

---

*Smith would win the Pulitzer Prize in 1964 for his reporting of the Kennedy assassination.

was still alive and on his way to a hospital. As the announcer talked, I could tell from the tone of his voice—beyond sadness, despairing—that it was true. This was my own "Where were you when President Kennedy died?" moment: I was in a car with my fiancé, about to experience a period of emotional numbness that was, for me, unprecedented.

My head was flooded with images of the President the last time I saw him, just seven days earlier, in the Carlyle. He had hugged me and said he'd call me when he got back from Texas. I looked over at Tony and saw a stranger—someone with whom I could never share these thoughts, these memories. I'd never told Tony a thing about our relationship. He'd never met him. Tony and I had no common ground to grieve about the President or even to talk about him. I suddenly felt isolated and walled off from the man I was about to marry.

The world rushed by outside the windows as we neared Southport, Connecticut. Tony reached over and squeezed my hand in sympathy but I hardly felt it. I opened the passenger car window and tried to breathe in the cool November air. More bulletins were coming in now. The President had been shot in the head.

I dreaded walking into the house and seeing my future in-laws. The Fahnestocks were staunch Republicans who made a sport out of disparaging the President, and their barbs got nastier when they had a drink in hand. The cocktail hour had already started when we pulled into their driveway off Sasco Creek Road at about four o'clock, but the President's death seemed to have a sobering effect even on them. Mr. Fahnestock gave me a long hug, which was unusual. He said something nice about the President, acknowledging that I knew him and that I might be suffering more than most people.

"We've opened the bar a little early today, Mimi," Mr. Fahnestock said.

He handed me a glass of Dewar's.

"This is what you need," he said.

The television set in the den was on, but Mr. and Mrs. Fahnestock seemed uninterested in further news. Tony's mother insisted that we sit and chat in their living room, which looked out over Southport Harbor, as if nothing had happened. It was bizarre. The most momentous event in a generation was receiving blanket coverage on television and radio, and my future in-laws coped with it by ignoring it. They preferred to make small talk about our wedding. I remember sitting there, but I didn't hear a word Mrs. Fahnestock said.

I struggled with my emotions that night. I wanted to get up and watch television. I wanted to know everything. My numbness had been replaced by a bottomless sense of loss, not only for myself but for all the people at the White House, especially Dave Powers. What would he do without the President? Meanwhile, we moved from the living room to the dining room for the traditional Friday-night roast chicken. It became nearly unbearable. I felt like I would break down in tears right at the table. My thoughts also turned to my parents, but speaking to them would have been an expensive long-distance call, so I abandoned the idea. I would be seeing them the next day, anyway.

At about nine-thirty the Fahnestocks finally went off to bed, taking their usual nightcaps with them. Tony and I went into the den and watched the television. He stretched out on the couch and I sat directly in front of the TV on the floor. Every network was carrying the news, endlessly playing the black-and-white footage of the President and Mrs. Kennedy arriving in Dallas, Mrs. Kennedy being given a bouquet of roses, the motorcade as it left the airport.

Mercifully, there was no footage of the actual shooting. (That, of course, would come later.) So network anchors such as Walter Cronkite resorted to showing photographs of the Kennedys smiling and laughing in the car, then the President clutching his throat as the second bullet passed through him and went on to wound Governor Connally. There was no image of the final shot, which shattered the President's head. The most indelible photograph from that day was of Lyndon Johnson taking the oath of office on Air Force One while Mrs. Kennedy stood beside him in her bloodstained suit. Cecil Stoughton took that famous photograph, the same White House photographer who had taken my engagement picture just two months before, as a personal favor.

I wasn't calm, but I wasn't losing control, either, even as we watched the live, grainy television images of Air Force One landing that night at Andrews Air Force Base, returning from Texas with the President's body. I heard Mr. Fahnestock come down the steps to refill his glass. "Just a splash," he said, as he looked in on us.

What Tony and I, as well as the entire nation, were watching was slow, mournful, and surreal. Only when I saw the coffin come off the plane did I finally accept that President Kennedy was gone. What sent me over the edge was the image of Dave Powers with his hand on the casket, standing in front of it as if he were guarding the President, then lifting it with other aides into the waiting Navy ambulance.

I remember getting up from the floor, standing off to the side between Tony and the TV. I was crying, looking back and forth from the TV screen to Tony, alternating between the image of the dead President and my fiancé.

My tears turned into violent, racking sobs, and Tony was concerned. As far as Tony knew, I was just someone who had spent two summers in the press office, so my reaction must have seemed extreme.

"Are you all right?" he said.

I shook my head.

"What's *happening* to you?" he said.

I couldn't answer. My eyes darted between the TV and Tony, as if I were watching a tennis match. It was disorienting. But I thought for sure that Tony could see through me and understand why I was crying. I thought for sure that it would finally dawn on him why he was at Fort Meade in Maryland, not in Louisiana—that he knew why the President interceded on his behalf. I was sure he was making a connection between that bit of favoritism and my relationship with the President. All the guilt I had been feeling about deceiving Tony was coming to a boil as I went back and forth between the sight of Tony relaxing on the couch and the images of JFK on the TV screen. My sense of guilt was expanding with each passing second. I was convinced that Tony not only saw it but comprehended it completely—and that it started the wheels of suspicion turning in his head.

He knows everything, I thought. *I have to come clean and be honest with him.* I was not thinking clearly. I'm sure of that. But I had no idea how the scene I was about to create would play out.

"There's something I have to tell you," I said.

"What?"

"The President . . ."

"What?" he interrupted.

"It's more than you think. . . ."

"What?"

"I'm not as innocent as you think."

"What?"

"There's a reason I quit school."

"What?"

"You have to let me finish, please."

I stopped crying and tried to gather my thoughts.

"I was closer to him. . . ."

"What are you telling me — that you slept with President Kennedy?"

I don't know how he made that leap from my distress to my infidelity, but I nodded yes, relieved that I didn't have to say the words out loud.

Then Tony's tone shifted into a harsh interrogation.

"Since when?" he asked.

"Last year."

"Even after you met me?"

I nodded.

"Even after we were *engaged*?"

I nodded again.

"How many times?"

"I don't know. A lot."

Then there was silence. I think Tony realized that the more questions he asked, the more pain he would be inflicting upon himself. A primal sense of self-protection kicked in, and he went quiet, turning away from me and staring at the TV.

I turned my back to him for a second, then spun around and returned to my place on the floor, near his feet, with my back against the sofa. I hoped he might put his hand on my shoulder, do something to comfort me, to tell me that he forgave me.

Of course, this was too much to hope for. (If our roles

had been reversed, I know I would not be so forgiving.) I absently gazed at the flickering TV screen, waiting for a consoling gesture that never came.

I had finally shared my secret with someone. But there was no catharsis, no relief. I had merely traded one problem for another, of possibly greater consequence. I had hurt Tony.

After a few minutes, Tony got up, turned off the TV, and said, "I'm going to bed."

Turning off the TV was a signal that I should be coming upstairs as well, but I couldn't move from the couch. I wanted to be alone and gather my thoughts. I tried to sort out what I had just done, and how it might affect Tony. I was terrified that I'd lost him, that the next morning he would call off our engagement. I went over the scene between us, reproaching myself for being so honest and blunt with him, for dropping the news on him so suddenly. I realized that maybe a better course would have been to hold on to my secret, to get a grip on myself and plan a more considered approach at a more appropriate moment, when it would be less of a bombshell — if it could ever be less of a bombshell. But the President's death and the crescendo of strange and powerful emotions I was feeling forced my hand. I couldn't suppress the truth. I had no choice but to tell Tony everything.

I had no idea what would happen next—or what Tony would say the next morning. Frankly, I wouldn't blame him for saying he never wanted to see me again.

We were sleeping in separate bedrooms at the Fahnestocks, as we had at my parents' house in New Jersey; such was the custom then for unmarried couples, even those who were engaged. I closed my door and lay on the bed, nowhere near sleep, my heart pounding. I was no longer thinking about President Kennedy—and the immense sadness of his death. I was fretting about the next twelve hours.

There was a bathroom connecting the guest room, where I was, and Tony's small bedroom. I heard the bathroom door open into my room and saw Tony standing in the doorway. Saying nothing, he yanked back the covers, climbed into my bed, and, without a word, initiated our first sexual encounter. I was so desperate to keep him, I didn't resist. It was forceful and clumsy—and I had no idea how to behave, neither how to express my sorrow at hurting him nor how to offer my love to heal the pain. He then left the bedroom as abruptly as he had entered it. I just lay there, dazed. I realize now he was laying claim to me, just as the President had done those many months before. It was sex, but there was no love.

The next morning was bizarre. Life with Tony as I had known it just twenty-four hours earlier had been tossed out the window, replaced instead by a brittle formality and awkwardness. At the breakfast table with his parents, we made small talk about wedding logistics and the weather. Incredibly, the subject of the President's assassination never came up.

Tony and I left after breakfast. He would drop me off at home in New Jersey and then continue on to Fort Meade. We drove in stony silence. As mile after mile ticked by, not once did Tony glance my way.

When we exited the Garden State Parkway, a few miles from my home, Tony abruptly pulled over at a bank of public telephones. For the first time since departing Southport, he spoke to me.

"Give me the phone number of the White House," he said.

I automatically rattled off the number—202 National

8-1414—not understanding why he wanted it or what he was going to do. He repeated the number to himself, got out of the car, and went to the phone. When he returned, he claimed he had told the press office that no one at the White House should ever contact me again.

I realize now he must have been lying. The President had just been killed. The White House switchboard was undoubtedly jammed with calls, and even if he had gotten through, I can't imagine anyone in the press office taking, let alone dignifying, a message from an angry stranger about little Mimi Beardsley. The press office was dealing with the death of one president and the first day in office of a new one; surely they had their hands full. But I was so traumatized at the time, I believed him.

Then the trauma became permanent.

As we sat on the side of the road, Tony added another punishing layer of secrecy to my affair with the President. He made it a condition of my marriage to him.

"You will never, ever say anything to anyone about what you told me last night," he said. "Not your parents or your sisters or brothers or friends. Nobody. Ever."

I had been holding back tears all morning, but with the combination of my guilt and Tony's anger and the fear that our wedding plans—my future life—were collapsing around me, I started sobbing.

"Do you hear me?" he said.

I was too upset to open my mouth. I stared ahead and nodded up and down in agreement.

"Good," he said.

I felt relieved as he pulled back onto the road. I took what he'd said to mean that if I obeyed him, then the wedding would go ahead. There would be no scandal, no disgrace, no tearful explanations of why the wedding had been canceled.

Tony had taken charge, and in a real sense, I was grateful. He wasn't going to let anything derail his plans, and his plan at the moment was to get married. For a long time I liked to think he was protecting me by demanding my silence, but I have come to realize that he was protecting only himself and his own ego. My revelation had embarrassed him. He must have hated the fact that the President had claimed me before he did. He must have felt humiliated that I continued to see the President after we met. He must have felt he'd never measure up to someone so charismatic and powerful. Perhaps he even felt I was mocking him. So his response was understandable. He was wounded.

But I, too, was in pain. The President I knew, admired, and, yes, even loved in my own misguided way, was dead, and I had nobody to talk to about him, no one with whom I could share my grief. And now I was being ordered to erase him from my life, to act as if he had never existed? I had already gotten a glimpse, the night before, of the dark force my secret could unleash in Tony. After all, I had told no one for a year and a half, and sharing it for the first time engendered nothing but anger, recrimination, sexual violence, and shame.

Is it any wonder I agreed so easily to Tony's demand?

I think often, even now, of that moment in the car. For years, I saw Tony's ultimatum, much like Dave Powers's second invitation to the President's residence, as another pivot point in my life. But only recently, in the process of writing this book, did I come to realize that it was a false one. And it was false because I didn't have any room to maneuver. Looking back on it, I see that I had only two options—agree to keep the secret or call off the engagement. It doesn't now, and didn't then, seem like much of a choice.

And what if I had never told Tony in the first place? I'm not sure that would have been possible, given how much distress I was in when I told him. But if I *had* managed it, I know enough now about the toxic effects of keeping a shameful secret to know that it would have eaten my insides on our wedding day, and on our honeymoon, and on the day I gave birth to our first child, and on every other momentous day in our marriage. Not telling him was not an option.

We might have talked it out more honestly and rationally. Tony and I, indeed, *should* have been able to talk about it, and if there ever was a time to do that, it was there in the car on the side of the road. It would have been the adult thing to do, certainly. I could have deflected his demand to keep silent and said, "We can't brush this under the rug. We need help with this. We need to talk about this." But we were so young—I was twenty and Tony was twenty-three—and we didn't have the emotional tools to address it. It didn't occur to either one of us then that burying the issue would not make it go away.

I can only imagine how devastated and betrayed Tony must have felt, and how the best way for him to deal with that pain was simply to delete it. For my part, I was feeling enormous insecurity and vulnerability. My biggest fear was the idea that I would fail at the simple act of getting married. Not only would I have to tell family and friends that the wedding was off, but how would I explain our sudden change of heart without mentioning the President?

So when Tony gave me an opening to save our engagement—all I had to do was never speak again about President

Kennedy—I seized on it immediately as a lifeline. This wasn't forgiveness. But it did let us move on. This is why I agreed to remain silent. If shutting out everything about the President would keep Tony in my life, and save me from embarrassment, I could live with that.

The next four days at my parents' house were dominated by nonstop coverage of the President's death on every TV channel. My younger sister and my parents stayed glued to the set in our pine-paneled library, but I did my best to avoid it. Instead, I helped my mother in the kitchen, preparing meals that everyone but me ate in front of the television. It was impossible to avoid catching glimpses of the enormous crowds passing the flag-draped coffin in the Capitol rotunda, the breaking news of Lee Harvey Oswald's murder in Dallas, the funeral procession in Washington to St. Matthew's Cathedral, brothers Bobby and Ted walking behind the horse-drawn caisson, little John's salute, Mrs. Kennedy's brittle face, hovering between crying and stoic grace, at Arlington National Cemetery while a twenty-one-gun salute sounded and Air Force One made a farewell flyover. But I willed myself to feel nothing as the heartbreaking images floated by. I didn't cry or shed a tear, not once.

If my mother and father were puzzled by my detachment and stoicism, they never said anything about it. They didn't ask me why I didn't even try to go to Washington to bear witness. Part of me, of course, desperately longed to be there, to grieve with all my friends at the White House. But I was determined to honor Tony's demand.

Tony, for his part, was completing his Army tour of duty, which kept us apart for a big chunk of the time before the wedding. But even when we were together, as much as I tried to deny it, the tenor of our relationship was different. We had always been light and playful with each other, as if we didn't have a care in the world. Now I felt a creeping unease with him, as if he was constantly scrutinizing me and finding me wanting. I attributed this to his justifiable anger but thought—hoped—that it would fade with time and the joy of our wedding and honeymoon.

Tony and I were married on January 4, 1964, at Christ Episcopal Church in Middletown, New Jersey. Our wedding photos show a happy, carefree young couple, smiling, dancing, feeding each other the traditional piece of cake. I had seven attendants, including my sister Buffy as maid of honor and Marnie Stuart, Kirk Dyett, and Wendy Taylor among my bridesmaids. I wore my mother's wedding dress, as our wedding announcement in *The New York Times* would note, of "ivory satin in modified Empire style with an heirloom rose point veil belonging to the bridegroom's maternal grandmother." I carried a bouquet of butterfly orchids. The bridesmaids carried pink roses and wore long, dark gowns of forest-green velvet, with bows of deeper green in their hair. All the groomsmen were listed, as were our boarding schools and colleges. Our grandparents were named. There was even a mention of the debutante balls where I had been "presented."

I had provided all the information to the newspaper for the announcement, so only I was aware that, among all the social details, there was a glaring omission about the bride: Whereas my engagement announcement a few months earlier had proudly noted that I had worked in the White House press office in 1962 and 1963, my wedding announcement made no mention of it. It was as if that part of my life had never happened.

Chapter Twelve

And just like that I was Mimi Fahnestock.

I not only took on Tony's name, I also took on all his ambitions for life. That meant settling in New York City, where, after his Army duty was up, he accepted a job at Morgan Guaranty. That meant setting up a home with him in a tiny apartment on East Seventy-eighth Street in Manhattan— a space so cramped I couldn't open the oven door in the kitchen if the refrigerator was open. That meant cooking for him every night and supporting his career and getting a job myself and saving money to buy a bigger apartment or a house in the suburbs. That also meant sharing the not-too-distant goal of starting a family.

We didn't talk deeply or frequently about these mutual goals. We were of such similar backgrounds that we just accepted them as part of the life we were meant to live. Although I was only twenty, I embraced these ambitions with the unquestioning enthusiasm of someone who had always pictured herself as a happy homemaker. In this self-image in 1964, I was not much different from the majority of young women in America; bra-burning protests were still four or

five years away. I was married and had my whole life in front
of me.

Our marriage lasted twenty-six years and can be divided,
with eerie precision, into two distinct halves. The first thirteen years were happy ones; the rest were not. As a result,
Tony and I divorced in 1990.

There are countless reasons marriages fail. And the reasons don't show up all at once. They accumulate as a couple
goes through the ups and downs of building a life, pursuing
careers, bringing children into the world and raising them
and sending them back into the world, defining and redefin-
ing their notion of how to love and be loved in return. In
some ways, Tony and I were no different from the millions of
couples out there who started with the best intentions but
grew apart over many years and eventually turned into
semi-hostile strangers in their own home.

For years I resisted pinning any blame for my failed marriage on my affair with JFK. I knew that telling Tony about
the relationship that dark day in November 1963 wasn't the
most auspicious or healthy way to begin a marriage, but I
never saw it as the thing that doomed our marriage from the
start. After all, we had thirteen good years, producing two
wonderful girls—and eventually six grandchildren. They are
beyond precious to me, and I cannot imagine my life without
them. So there's that to be said for our marriage: It created
most of what I hold dear.

Years after the divorce, though, when I was a single
woman on my own in Manhattan, I began to reconsider the
impact that revealing my secret had on our marriage. I
thought that given the happy years we shared, it was behind
us. But I came to accept that my affair with JFK and Tony's
demand that I bury the subject forever were like two patho-
gens that we introduced into our marriage and that slowly,

painfully, led to its death. Tony was never able to trust me
completely after that day, and for good reason. Nothing could
erase the depth of his hurt. He carried that baggage for our
entire marriage. It was forever woven into the emotional fabric of our lives together, and I could sense it. The anger and
jealousy never completely disappeared.

I blame both of us for that. If we could have found a way
to talk openly—and if we hadn't had to treat the affair as a
mark of my shame and Tony's humiliation—then the secret's
poisonous power might have dissolved over time.

The wise and mature thing to do—had I been wiser and
more mature at this point in my life—would have been to
confront Tony. I should have challenged him to make a
choice: "What do you want to do?" I could have said. "Hold
on to this anger for the rest of our lives?"

I should have tried to make him appreciate that in that
moment of utter confusion and grief when I exposed myself
to him in his parents' den, it was not only a gesture of honesty but one of faith as well—in him and his love for me. I
should have reminded him that time heals most wounds and
that it's sometimes the most disastrous marital events—an
awful family visit, a nightmarish vacation, a forgotten birthday, or some other breakdown in our expectations—that,
over time, inspire the fondest and funniest memories in the
retelling. If we could put this behind us, perhaps years later
we could marvel over—even laugh about—the time when
Tony's wife had an affair with the President of the United
States when she was very, very young.

If only to maintain my dignity, maybe I should have
drawn a line in the sand and said, "If you can't forgive me,
you shouldn't marry me."

But I never said any of that. Not only that, I didn't even
think it. I didn't have the self-confidence to assert myself

with such a potentially devastating ultimatum. I didn't have the maturity to see the toxic emotional climate my silence — our silence — would create in our marriage.

Instead, I went about blithely purging any evidence of JFK from my existence, pretending it hadn't happened. It wasn't enough that my White House internship had been expunged from my wedding announcement. It wasn't enough that I could never refer to my internship or mention the Kennedy name around Tony and our friends. It wasn't enough that I made an effort to avoid reading or watching anything about JFK.* Even my private thoughts had to be controlled. If I allowed the President to pop into my mind or spent any time reflecting about my relationship with him, I believed it was like cheating on Tony. Guilt was always nipping at my heels.

When Tony and I had gotten married, I had hidden away, in various places around our apartment, the three gifts from the President: the gold-and-diamond pins he gave me upon my engagement, the gray suit from Bloomingdale's, and the photograph he had signed when I left Washington. As a few months passed and my feelings of guilt deepened, I came to see these gifts as evidence of a crime. And what do you do with evidence of a crime? You dispose of it.

I did it all in one day, in 1964, while Tony was at work. I was going to secretarial school at the time, sharpening the

---

*This wasn't so easy to do in late 1964. Seven days after JFK's death, President Johnson had established the Warren Commission to investigate the assassination. The Commission issued its 888-page report in September 1964, creating instant controversy (which persists to this day) and immediately thrusting JFK's name and image everywhere again.

typing and shorthand skills that had been in such short supply during my stint at the White House. I hadn't found a job yet, so I had time during the day.

I took the suit to a thrift shop along Second Avenue on the Upper East Side and, feeling a twinge of regret at sacrificing the most extravagant piece of clothing I owned, quietly handed it to the woman behind the counter.

"What's the matter, dear?" I remember her asking as she looked it over. "It looks brand-new. Doesn't it fit anymore?"

I stared blankly at her, saying nothing.

Next were the gold-and-diamond pins. At first I considered tossing them down the incinerator chute in the hallway outside our apartment, but as I opened the chute door, I couldn't bring myself to treat them as trash. They were too beautiful. I took them to a pawn shop on Twenty-third Street and Second Avenue, and handed them over, fighting back tears. I don't recall how much the pawnbroker offered me, but I do remember that I was in no mood to bargain with him. I folded the cash in my purse and tossed the pawn ticket away as soon as I stepped outside. When it was done, I felt a strong sense of relief. I told myself I was fulfilling a duty to my husband.

The last piece to go was the photograph. I felt such tenderness when I pulled it out from its hiding spot behind other pictures in a photo album. I took one last look at the image of the President, on his boat in a blue polo shirt and white khakis, his right hand on the wheel, as he smiled into the sun. I traced my fingers over the inscription: "To Mimi, with warmest regards and deep appreciation." I recalled his mischievous conspiratorial tone when, upon finishing it, he'd looked at me and said, "Only you and I know what that really means."

I pulled a pair of scissors from the drawer and cut it into a hundred tiny pieces.

I was so frantic and upset and paranoid about this photo—and the intimacy it called up—that I suddenly was overcome by a wild fear that someone might piece it together again. Tossing the pieces in a wastebasket or even the incinerator wouldn't protect me. So I gathered them into a small gift bag and went out onto the street, where I parceled them out among several different trash cans around the neighborhood. If anyone wanted to trace the photo back to me, they'd have to dig through a lot of trash and use a lot of Scotch tape.

Then I returned to the apartment and sat in the living room, waiting for Tony to come home. I must have believed that in ridding myself of the last vestiges of JFK, everything would be all right again. Tony would never come across them accidentally, not now. He could never confront me with questions that would lead back to my betrayal. I would not have to face the possibility of his anger. I had done the right thing for both of us. Or so I thought.

That evening when Tony came home, he poured himself a drink and gave me a peck on the cheek. I asked about his day, and we settled into pleasant, banal small talk about his job. The safety I had imagined wasn't there, of course. I couldn't talk about what I had done that day, and the cloud still hovered.

In a larger sense, this became the prevailing pattern in our marriage. Whenever something important needed to be discussed, if there was an event that carried any emotional resonance that needed to be hashed out honestly, we would avoid it.

Again, it's important to remember how young we were at the time. We were twenty and twenty-three, kids playing at being adults, following the script: Tony would be the provider and I the homemaker. Even in our emotional makeup, we were following patterns set by our parents. We didn't share what we felt. (Employing a word like *share* to reveal our feelings wasn't even in our vocabulary back then.) Painful circumstances were dealt with stoically; the goal was always to overcome rather than to discuss or understand. The solution to any hardship lay in *not* letting it hurt or damage us— not letting it touch us at all.

I know this now with the wisdom of hindsight, but I don't mean to suggest I was trapped for all twenty-six years in a life of existential despair. The fact is, I was happy being a new bride. I was full of high spirits—and I still carried with me the residual glow that came with the security of being married and in love. As we started out, Tony and I were surrounded by friends from boarding school and college days who were also beginning their careers in Manhattan. Most weeknights, with the boundless energy of twentysomethings, we would assemble as a pack at a bar or at an impromptu party at one of our apartments, and on weekends we would visit my parents in New Jersey. It was a fun time, which may have masked the emotional missteps Tony and I were making. It's also why I see it only in hindsight. Back then, I was distracted by youth and the promise of a perfect life. I believed everything would always work out. Today, I know better.

A few weeks after purging the JFK gifts, in June 1964, I found out I was pregnant. It was unexpected but happy news for us. Our only concern was our finances. We would need a bigger apartment, with a second bedroom for the baby, and we would need to do all this solely on Tony's salary. I had just landed my first full-time job with, of all things, the New York

State Republican Committee (an indicator of how fully I had suppressed my involvement with JFK's Democratic administration), and I worried how my pregnancy would play with my new employers. I fully intended to keep working right up to my due date in February 1965 — we needed the money — and then devote myself to motherhood.

It didn't work out that way.

In my seventh month of pregnancy, we were at my parents' house in New Jersey when I suddenly went into labor in the middle of the night. After being rushed by ambulance to Riverview Hospital in nearby Red Bank, our little boy, Christopher Snowden Fahnestock, was born in an emergency room in the early hours of December 6, 1964, eight weeks prematurely. He died the following day of the same underdeveloped lung syndrome that had taken the life of Patrick Bouvier Kennedy the year before. Even in my grief, I appreciated the coincidence. I don't know if Tony had similar thoughts, because I never remember us actually talking about the baby, or our loss. The wound was too fresh and painful — and what would be the point? I don't blame Tony for that. I've known other couples who've lost a baby or young child who also can't ever bring themselves to mention the subject. But to me, our silence about Christopher was yet another example of how, in our neediest moments, we were unable to comfort each other.

Everything about that time fills me with sadness now. The worst part may have been the strange hours between the baby's birth and death. Dr. Small, the obstetrician who delivered Christopher, had told me his life would be very short, a matter of a day or two. Knowing the baby was going to die, he thought it was important for me to see Christopher. He helped me walk down the hallway to the nursery window and pointed out my new son in a back row bassinet behind the healthy full-term babies who were featured in front. I strained to get a glimpse of him, but he was too far away. It is the single saddest moment of my life—that I didn't get to see Christopher or hold him. Neither was I able to say goodbye. I was still recovering in the hospital when my mother and Tony arranged a small graveside service and buried Christopher in our family plot at Fairview Cemetery in Middletown, New Jersey. I still visit the spot, marked by a modest tombstone, always wishing I could have held him just once.

No mother ever gets over the death of a child. When I look at pictures of me from the weeks immediately after the baby's death, the contrast with the happy-go-lucky bride of a year earlier is shocking. My face and body are puffy with the added weight of pregnancy. My eyes are lifeless orbs. And the down-turned corners of my mouth made me look like I'd forgotten how to smile.

As hard as it was, I tried valiantly to pull myself together. I went back to work as soon as I could, trying not to burden people with my problems. And slowly the sadness lifted to where I could appreciate my life again. I had a new apartment with a second bedroom that Tony converted into an office. He was doing well at work—and soon we would be moving to Cambridge, Massachusetts, because he'd decided to pursue his MBA at Harvard Business School.

It would be a fresh start—something that I badly needed.

Tony had many virtues, and in Cambridge they came to the fore. He had always done well at school. He was ambitious, smart, conscientious, not afraid of hard work. He also thrived on control—and was never happier than when he was planning a course of action and carrying it through. He devoured his case studies and loved a challenge. It made perfect sense that he would go after an MBA at the premier business school in the country. At Harvard, Tony was in heaven.

This love of control and order came in handy for him not only in the workplace and at business school but in our family life as well. I recall visiting my parents in New Jersey with Tony about three years into our marriage. They had just sold Still Pond Farm, the house my siblings and I had grown up in, and my father and mother were struggling with decisions about money and where to live. They were not rich by any means, and they were moving into their retirement years.

One afternoon, as we ate lunch in a diner in Seabright, my father launched into a gloomy tale about how things were so bad he could no longer afford to keep our family dog, a black Labrador named Notso. They were looking for a home for him, he said. The conversation was so depressing, I started to cry—which always made Tony anxious. Tony respected my father—addressing him as "Mr. B.," never by Randy—but at this moment, he put the niceties aside and took charge.

"Mr. B., pull yourself together," he said. "You don't need to get rid of Notso. You need a plan, and you need to stick to it."

He was only twenty-six, but he was acting like a parent. He grilled my mom and dad about their assets and expenses, and proved to them that they were more than capable of taking care of a dog, not to mention many other things they claimed they could not afford. I had seen this fierce side of Tony before—namely, on the night of November 22, 1963— and it often frightened me; it was a big reason I opted for silence rather than confrontation around him. But on that day, I saw how the part of him that so cowed me could also be such a comfort.

Tony was in his element at Harvard Business School, and because he was happy, I was happy. We had taken out a loan to cover his tuition, but it was up to me to cover our living expenses. Through my New York Republican contacts, I had landed a job as a secretary in the office of the Massachusetts attorney general, a courtly, bespectacled public servant named Elliot Richardson (who in October 1973 would famously resign as Richard Nixon's attorney general rather than carry out the order to fire Watergate special prosecutor Archibald Cox). It was serious work but with none of the Camelot glamour or sense of fun—and certainly none of the extracurricular hijinks. I never told anyone in the office that I had been a White House intern for two summers, and I purposely kept it off my résumé.

We rented a small apartment in a big clapboard house on Gerry Street, a stone's throw from the Charles River and a quick walk to the Harvard campus. It was a time of great political upheaval at Harvard—and across the country—but Tony and I remained so focused on our plan—Tony on his studies, me on making sure we could pay our bills—that the "revolution" barely touched us. We were so conservative and square. A few blocks away, students with long hair and dressed in Army surplus were protesting the Vietnam War, while Tony wore his white button-down shirts and crew-neck sweaters and blue blazers to school and I put on my prim blouses and skirts to work for a Republican who was the state's chief law enforcement officer. Instead of smoking marijuana, we smoked cigarettes. Instead of manning the barricades, we holed up in our apartment. I would come home late from work and put together a casserole or Tony's favorite meal of a burger with a wedge of iceberg lettuce and Russian dressing. We couldn't afford to go out to dinner, and we didn't socialize much. Tony would study at his desk, and I would curl up on a sofa with a book. Michael Ansara, a well-known political activist and one of the founders of Harvard's SDS chapter, lived in one of the adjacent apartments, but I don't recall saying a word to him in the two years that we lived there.

It wasn't exactly a wild time for us, but there was a renewed sense of romance in our relationship, as Tony and I were in sync as a couple. We were unified in our commitment to our life plan. Tony would get his MBA and we would return to New York, where he would take a coveted job in finance. We were so in sync, in fact, that with one small exception (which I'll get to shortly), I never thought about President Kennedy. This was all the more extraordinary when you consider that we were living in Harvard, where the most famous alumnus at the time was surely JFK. John F. Kennedy Park, the Kennedy School of Government, and J. F. Kennedy Street could all be found less than one thousand yards from our apartment door. If I had wanted to avoid memories of JFK, the Boston area was most assuredly *not* the place to do it; it was practically a Kennedy theme park.

Three years had passed since the death of little Christopher. Even though Tony was still a student and I was making a modest secretary's salary, we were determined to have a baby, which we finally did on September 22, 1968, a few weeks after Tony began his second year at school. Our daughter Lisa was healthy and perfect, and I loved everything about taking care of her, even diaper duty and midnight feedings. On Lisa's first outing, I pushed her blue pram over to Brattle Street and cajoled the owner of our drugstore to come out to the street "to see what I had gotten." Those were the words I used, as if Lisa was the most precious gift I had ever received. Suddenly, my life was centered on her, and I didn't mind for a second.

My secret, of course, stayed deeply buried.

And yet on a crisp spring day in 1969 when I took an afternoon walk with the baby in the carriage, I passed a hair salon on Massachusetts Avenue advertising Frances Fox hair products in the window. It had been six years since I'd given the President his regular hair treatments, but suddenly I was overcome with emotion. I looked both ways down the street to make sure no one was watching me (ridiculous, I know) and, carrying Lisa in my arms, walked into the store to see which products they sold. I wasn't planning to buy anything. I just wanted to luxuriate in the warm memory of President Kennedy, if only for a few minutes. I picked up the bottles and turned them over in my hands. I carefully set them back on the counter and walked out. I felt so guilty about what I'd done, I tucked the incident away, deep in my mind. I wasn't going to mention it. Lisa, barely six months old, wasn't talking either.

Tony got his MBA in June 1969 and, as we had hoped, was recruited by Goldman Sachs for a well-paying job in New York. At first, we rented a carriage house in Greenwich, Connecticut, thinking that a leafy suburb was a better place to raise our new family. But after nine months of commuting, Tony was ready to return to the city. I was, too. I missed the energy of city street life. One of Tony's colleagues suggested Brooklyn Heights, a neighborhood on the other side of the East River, directly across from Wall Street. The only thing I knew about the borough of Brooklyn was that my father had been born there. To our amazement it took us only one weekend, armed with the local paper, to find an exquisite floor-through garden apartment on tree-lined Hicks Street. Tony was delighted with his one-stop subway ride to his office, and I fell in love with the community. It was the city but "not too much" city. I had a beautiful baby in my arms and a great provider of a husband by my side. Life was good.

Chapter Thirteen

Between November 1963, when I told Tony about JFK, and May 2003, when the *Daily News* exposed my secret, there were only a few other people with whom I shared the story of my affair. I had spent my young adult life trying to be a perfect wife and mother. Of course, that didn't mean I was happy. But I hid my unhappiness behind a placid façade, a skill at which I excelled. To family and friends I appeared dutiful, capable, energetic, and content, but as hard as I tried to keep it up, cracks in the façade inevitably appeared.

In the summer of 1973, I told my secret to my cousin Joan Ellis. I had just turned thirty. My second daughter, Jenny, had been born three years after her sister and was just learning to walk and talk. Along with Lisa, she was bathed in the constant attention of her doting parents. Tony's career had blossomed at Goldman Sachs to the point where, just before Jenny's birth, we had been able to afford a three-bedroom apartment in one of Brooklyn Heights well-established coop buildings, along with a summer rental in Rumson, New Jersey.

The summer house was beautifully furnished, on top of

a hill at the end of a long stone driveway, an hour from the city. The only thing it lacked was a television, which was a problem in the summer of 1973 when the entire nation was transfixed by the Watergate scandal. Nearly every day the networks would pre-empt their usual programming to show the Senate hearings chaired by North Carolina senator Sam Ervin. I was as mesmerized as everyone else by this unprecedented episode of political high drama. Most days, while Tony was at work, I would pile the girls and our babysitter in the car and drive the few miles to my cousin Joan's house, where her television was sure to be tuned to the hearings.

Joan was twelve years older than I. Years before moving back to New Jersey to start their own electronics company and raise their three children, Joan and her husband had worked in Washington, D.C. In addition to being the smartest woman I knew, Joan was also the most private. She didn't gossip. She kept to herself and made a point of steering clear of the suburban social scene. If there was one person in my life who could appreciate the power of a secret, it was my cousin Joan.

The hearing that third week in July had been extraordinary. Alexander Butterfield had just revealed the existence of sophisticated audio taping equipment in the Oval Office, meaning that every conversation involving President Nixon had been recorded. I remember Joan and I took a break from the hearings while the babysitter put my daughters down for a nap. In need of fresh air, we decided to head over to nearby Sandy Hook State Park. We were walking along a deserted section of beach, musing about how damaging these tapes might be to President Nixon and how long he could keep their contents secret.

"Secrets," Joan said. "They always catch up with you."

Maybe that was the trigger. Maybe it was the fact that during that summer—living in this beautiful house, with my adorable daughters and successful husband—I was as content and fulfilled as I had ever been. Maybe I felt secure enough in my marriage that breaking my promise to Tony, just this once, didn't seem like such a big deal. Maybe it was the simple fact that we were discussing Washington and the presidency. Maybe it was the fact that I trusted Joan completely and could tell her anything. I had always admired her.

"I know," I said. "I've been keeping a secret myself."

And then I told her.

The most amazing thing is that the sky didn't fall. I wasn't struck by lightning. I didn't feel any more ashamed or guilty or sluttish. I actually felt better.

Joan was terrific, as I had hoped she would be. She had gone to Vassar with Jackie Kennedy, and was an ardent admirer of all things Camelot. But she didn't press me with prurient questions. She didn't profess shock or amazement. She just took it all in and said, "Well, that's going to make an interesting story for your grandkids someday." Her positive response cemented our kinship to this day.

As Joan and I drove back to her house to pick up my girls, I was glad I had told her but unsure if I would ever have the nerve to tell anyone else. The one thing I was sure about was that I wouldn't tell Tony that I had broken my promise.

It would be ten years before I shared my secret again. A new crack in my façade had been forming slowly, almost imperceptibly, during that first full decade of motherhood and marriage.

In 1976, Tony and I had bought a three-story fixer-upper

of a house at 19A Garden Place, one of the most desirable streets in Brooklyn Heights. It required extensive renovation, which I knew could either bring Tony and me closer together or push us further apart. I had taken courses at the New York School of Interior Design and been certified, so I took charge of all the details while the four of us lived for a year among plaster dust and workmen and exposed plumbing and missing appliances. The strain did not bring my husband closer to me. When things went awry, he would jump in the car, drive to New Jersey, and spend the night at the small house that we rented for weekends and summers.

The renovation in 1977, as silly as it sounds, was the emotional dividing line in my marriage. We'd had thirteen good years, and now we were about to have thirteen bad ones. It's not often that one can isolate a single moment when the love goes out of a marriage. But I can.

That summer, we had been invited by friends to their farmhouse in Tenants Harbor, Maine, as an escape valve from the renovation. Our hosts plied us with lobster dinners and cold drinks and endless board games. I remember being struck by the contrast in our hosts' affectionate, playful relationship with each other and the blank, practically lifeless relationship I had with Tony. The giveaway was our last morning in Maine, when I woke up and Tony abruptly turned away in bed, as if to announce that he'd rather be with anyone but me. That's when I finally admitted to myself that I wanted to be anywhere but with him.

From that moment I saw Tony only through a negative lens—and he did the same with me. I began keeping this horrible, mental running list of his shortcomings—how we didn't make love anymore, how he refused to accompany the kids and me on visits to my mother in Florida, how we didn't have any activities in common, how we never talked, how he didn't help around the house. This kind of resentment is never good, but I did something even worse with it: I turned it on myself. I wanted to know what I had done wrong—and how to fix myself. While the girls were at school and Tony was at work, I would surround myself at the kitchen table with the classic self-help books of the time, such as Gail Sheehy's *Passages* and M. Scott Peck's *The Road Less Traveled*, and less famous but even more trenchant books such as Harriet Lerner's *The Dance of Anger*. I would scribble in the margins and highlight passages that spoke to my situation. When I retrieved my copies to write this book, I saw that all my notes centered on the same issue—that "mutual loving confrontation" is the key to a meaningful relationship, that without it the relationship is shallow and doomed. Everything I read reminded me that I had been too passive in my marriage, too walled off, but I had neither the self-confidence nor the skill to assert myself.

How ironic that every evening, just before Tony came home, I would scramble to put away my books about "meaningful confrontation" so he couldn't see them, so he couldn't tell me once again to get my act together, as if I was just being weak. Eventually, the low point of my day became the moment I heard his key in our front gate, signaling his return home.

What saved me, literally, was running. I had finally quit smoking in the late seventies and took up running as a way of getting back in shape and achieving some kind of happiness. I don't know what took me so long to rekindle the love of running that I'd had as the only girl on the boys' track team at Rumson Country Day, but the first time I ran on the Promenade along the East River near my house, I knew this was something I could be good at.

Running immediately became the routine that lent a

tincture of inner peace to my life. I'd get up at five-thirty A.M. before Lisa and Jenny woke up, pull on my gray sweatpants, gulp down a cup of coffee, and head out for at least a four-mile run, sometimes more, down the Promenade, then onto the Brooklyn Bridge, to Manhattan and back, often catching sunrise over the East River, returning in time to get the girls off to school. The next morning I'd do it again.

This was a moment when the entire nation seemed to discover the joys of running. Jim Fixx's 1977 book *The Complete Book of Running* was the number-one bestseller for more than a year. It wasn't unusual to see runners of all shapes, ages, and sizes gathered in packs of ten or more, clad in their short shorts and Nikes, at a street corner as they headed out for a communal run before or after work. Pretty soon, I was one of those people. I joined the New York Road Runners Club, the biggest runners' group in America, and committed myself to running a marathon. Where my identity a year earlier had been wife and mother, it was now mother and *runner*.

I ran my first New York City Marathon in 1979 in four hours, sixteen minutes. I was proud to finish, and immediately began training for another one, vowing to break four hours (which I did). Before long, I was volunteering at the NYRRC and discovering a whole new circle of friends that had nothing to do with my sour domestic life in Brooklyn, and with whom I had so much in common. Tony tolerated the hours I spent running and didn't complain about them. My daughters heartily approved, and even seemed proud of me. After I finished a particularly long run on our weekends in New Jersey, the three of us would jump in the car and retrace my fifteen- or sixteen-mile route on the odometer. The mileage check would always end with a visit to the local

Dairy Queen (which may explain why the girls were so sup-portive of my running), where we would order large vanilla soft-serve cones with sprinkles.

In February 1981, I took a part-time job at the NYRRC, developing their research library. The pay barely exceeded the minimum wage, but I didn't care. My colleagues were all runners and, frankly, I hadn't felt this kind of excitement and sense of purpose since I was in the White House. I was par-ticularly drawn to a senior staffer named Bill Noel. He and I would train together, eat lunch together, and find a reason to visit each other's desk several times a day. Our flirtatious re-lationship was fueled by our mutual love of running and the feeling of accomplishment and good health it gave us.

When Bill had the bright idea that we should run the London Marathon in May 1982, I immediately said yes. Five of us flew over, but only he and I had signed up to run. The other three were along as tourists and supporting players, which explains why Bill and I were assigned to share a hotel room the night before the race. We needed the sleep; the others could go out and hit the town. It was a sign of how innocent our relationship was—and how committed we were to our sport—that no one in our group thought the sleeping arrangements were inappropriate, including us. By that time, I had not been intimate with my husband for five years. In fact, we'd barely hugged. Alone in the hotel room that night, I realized how much I yearned for physical affection and connection. So I made a bold, spontaneous gesture that sur-prised both of us. I climbed into Bill's bed instead of mine. It seemed like such a natural culmination of all the encourage-ment we'd shared during our months of training. I had turned thirty-nine two days before, and Bill was my third lover.

I had no regrets the next morning as we rode the train to the race's starting line in Greenwich Park (I finished in a personal best of three hours, twenty-seven minutes). The guilt wouldn't fully take hold until I was on the plane back to New York, and facing the prospect of seeing Tony again. As the reality of my infidelity sank in, I couldn't avoid one obvious fact: After years of accumulated silence with Tony, my marriage was crumbling.

So there I was, sitting in the living room of my comfortable home in Brooklyn Heights with my younger sister, Deb, in 1983. Deb's wedding had taken place in my home the year before. We were reminiscing about the ceremony when the conversation veered into a frank discussion of men. It was our first sisterly talk about sex, which prompted me to confess about my tryst with Bill. Deb was surprised to hear that I was the one who instigated it. The image of me jumping into another man's bed—in other words, asserting myself—was unexpected, out of character, a side of me she'd never seen. My experience was so different from hers, besides. She'd had many boyfriends before marrying at age thirty-three.

"I'm just amazed that, before Bill, you confined yourself to one man," she said.

"That's not quite true," I replied. "When I was working in Washington in the sixties, I had an affair with a married man."

"It was JFK, wasn't it?" she said.

"How'd you know?"

"Just a hunch," she said. "That's his reputation, isn't it?"

I was so taken aback by her intuition—as if she now saw the truth about me, as if maybe it was obvious all along—that I didn't feel the need to go into detail. I focused on how Tony had forbidden me from ever bringing it up, which Deb found puzzling. "Then why are you telling me?" she asked. I didn't have a ready answer and, mercifully, she dropped the subject. I think both of us were relieved. She knew how unhappy I was, and what more was there to say?

I kept working at the NYRRC for three more years. Bill and I continued to train and race together—from 10K races to triathlons—until injury and surgery converted me into a casual runner. Sometimes I would daydream about a life with Bill, though he never even held that out as a possibility. Whatever fantasies I had harbored about us ended when I accepted a full-time job as manager of a local tennis and squash club and, ever so slowly, drifted away from the world of runners and back into my unhappy marriage.

For the rest of the eighties, I didn't think about telling the secret to anyone. In fact, living in our crumbling marriage was so painful that I hardly shared anything with my friends or family. Tony and I barely acknowledged each other—and that emotional unavailability to each other was also hurting our teenage daughter Jenny. She resented both of us, but she lashed out at me because I was the easier target.

"You are the poorest excuse for a mother," she screamed at me one day.

I don't remember what inspired Jenny's tirade, but it was a brutal wake-up call, one of those moments that cut you to the core. She saw me as I was—a hollow woman incapable of standing up for herself. I thought about it all day as I ran errands in Manhattan. It was a Friday in April 1989. Tony was coming home early so he could go to New Jersey for the weekend. I walked down Madison Avenue to Grand Central

Terminal, entering from the west entrance off Vanderbilt Avenue. I stood at the top of the stairs, looking down at the commuters scurrying like ants, then up at the Kodak Colorama across the lobby. There was an enormous romantic scene of a couple holding hands on a tropical beach. Clichéd though it was, all I could see was love, and it made me profoundly sad because I couldn't imagine a future for myself with any romantic love in it. The tears began.

I've always thought Aha moments are supposed to be quiet insights, the result of peaceful meditation or a flash of brilliance. They're not supposed to be violent. But this one hit me hard, like a punch in the stomach. Right then I knew I had to end my marriage. I'd never felt such a strong sense of resolve.

When I got home, Tony was standing in the kitchen, talking on the phone to friends in New Jersey, making plans for getting away that weekend. I stood in the doorway, staring at him, counting the seconds until he noticed me. As he twisted the long yellow cord of the wall unit around his hand, he held up his index finger—his signal for me to wait a minute. Finally, he hung up and looked at me with an impatient expression.

"I want a divorce," I said.

"What?" he asked.

"I think you heard me." I wasn't going to say anything more. I waited for him to respond.

"Are you sure?" he said. "You've never known what you wanted, but if that's it, then that's what you'll get. I think you're going to regret it."

His words hung in the air, more a threat than an attempt to change my mind. He was right, in a way. I didn't know exactly what I wanted, but I knew I had to take a step toward change. I knew that Tony wasn't solely to blame for my un-happiness or the ruin of our marriage. It was my fault as much as his. I had not made his life happy. But I also knew that I had reached an endpoint to the misery we created for each other.

Tony was furious, but it wasn't in him to sulk or fester in anger; he immediately started making a plan. He bought an apartment on Willow Street nearby, while I stayed in our Garden Place home. We both hired lawyers, and after twelve months of acrimonious negotiations, we were no longer man and wife.

A few months later, in summer 1991, I was recounting the details of the divorce to my closest friend from Farmington, Marnie Pillsbury. She had been Marnie Stuart when, with Wendy Taylor, we shared a floor-through apartment in Georgetown my second summer as an intern.

We had gotten together for dinner because Marnie wanted to perform one of her periodic checkups on my well-being. She was and is that kind of friend.

Marnie was very patient as we conducted a postmortem on my twenty-six years of marriage. I told Marnie that screw-ing up the courage to end the marriage in 1989 had actually not been that difficult for me.

In some ways I had no choice. Marnie refused to accept that it was years of attrition that had forced two people apart.

"There must have been something bigger than that," she said.

"Well . . ." I hesitated. I had resisted telling Marnie for so many years, my natural instinct was to maintain the status quo. But then I realized that I wasn't married to Tony any-more. My marriage vow was obsolete. So was my promise to bury my secret.

Marnie didn't say a word as I played back the affair with President Kennedy. She was the best kind of friend, the kind who listens and doesn't feel she has to offer a solution to every problem. Sometimes all we want is for another person to hear us.

As for me, I savored the opportunity to finally tell a friend who had known me back then in my intern days. I felt that I was not only liberating the adult me but the nineteen-year-old me as well. It felt good.

Bit by bit, I was peeling away the layers. The next time I shared my secret was in the aftermath of Jacqueline Onassis's death on May 19, 1994. I was having dinner with K. C. Hyland, a friend and Wheaton College classmate, on Manhattan's Upper East Side. K.C. had walked over from the West Side through Central Park and happened upon the swarm of reporters and adoring fans who were standing vigil outside Mrs. Onassis's apartment at 1040 Fifth Avenue. It had been two days since Mrs. Onassis had died, and they were waiting for the occasional briefings on the funeral arrangements that her son, John F. Kennedy, Jr., provided.

Knowing that I had worked in the Kennedy White House, K.C. brought up Jackie's death over dinner and asked me if I had ever met her.

"No, never," I said, and then I described my attempt to interview Jackie while I was at Miss Porter's, which led to my internship.

"You must feel terrible about Jackie's death," she said.

"I do," I said, "but it's really reminding me of the President."

"What's that about?" she asked.

And so I told her.

It was four years after my divorce. I had just turned fifty. K.C., recently separated, and I had shared many walks in Central Park and dinners together. Our intimate talks covered just about all the topics single women in Manhattan would touch on—work, family, and, of course, men. It was natural and comfortable to tell her my secret that evening, everything from swimming in the pool, to cooking scrambled eggs, to traveling on trips and staying over at the White House. She was stunned at first but regrouped to press me for more details. She was particularly interested in the logistics—the how, where, and when; how we dealt with the First Lady; what role did the Secret Service play, et cetera. I talked nonstop for two hours. No doubt I had some residual fear that it wasn't right to be revealing so much detail (old habits die hard with a thirty-year secret). But K.C. was so interested in the minutiae and in my portrait of the President that it mostly felt healthy to let it all out.

Afterward, K.C. told me that she felt honored that I shared my secret with her, and "heavy with responsibility," as she put it, "to not tell a soul."

She got it. She appreciated the burden I had carried for so many years. So much of what we do and how we think is driven by our need to be understood by others. In sharing my secret with her, I had finally been understood.

The final person I told was my boss, Dr. Thomas K. Tewell, senior pastor at Fifth Avenue Presbyterian Church. He was a trained professional at dealing with confessors. He was also a man of wisdom whom I admired greatly. And he was a friend whom I felt comfortable calling Tom.

The year was 2000, the final year of the Clinton presidency and two years after the Monica Lewinsky scandal had erupted. By then I had been working at the church for five years, running their audio ministry, which meant I produced and marketed the audios and videos of any public activities at the church.

Fifth Avenue Presbyterian is not a humble white-steepled house of worship on a side road in the suburbs. It's a major brownstone edifice five blocks north of St. Patrick's Cathedral on one of Manhattan's busiest corners. Tom was a gifted speaker, and he geared his Sunday sermons to appeal to a big audience, not just church members but strangers passing by.

His sermon on February 13, part of his survey of the Ten Commandments, focused on the Seventh Commandment—"Thou shalt not commit adultery"—and his title, "Sex Is a Twelve-Letter Word," was sure to be a crowd-grabber.

That Sunday morning, the downstairs pews and upstairs balcony were standing-room-only. I set my recording machines on automatic and took a seat in the sanctuary. I didn't do this often, but I wanted to hear this message in person (and I was curious about that twelve-letter word). It turned out to be *faithfulness*. Tom's theme was that if you wanted to pursue a life of faithfulness in the way God intended, you must pay attention to three principles. Principle number one was that human sexuality is a sacred gift and must be exercised with great care. Sex is not a game. Principle number two was that God is not a prude. He doesn't want to rob us of pleasure, but promiscuity destroys relationships. Someone always gets hurt. Principle number three asserted that the deepest desire of the human spirit is for intimacy. Sex without intimacy is not faithfulness.

It's hard to argue with these principles, and Tom reinforced them with stories, some funny, some disturbing. One of them hit me hard. He said, "Sex makes headlines. We are bombarded by the scandalous headlines. We all know the names, and we know the stories—the congressmen, the judges, the athletes, the entertainers, and the pastors, and, yes, even the President of the United States, not just the current one, but the stories go back through history of presidents who were involved with women who were not their wives."

A good sermon reveals the truth; a great sermon does it in unexpected ways. And this one surprised me. At first I thought Tom was speaking directly to me, but he was mostly referencing the Clinton-Lewinsky affair and highlighting how it had hurt more than one or two people.

I have never felt more self-conscious sitting there in the sanctuary. It was as if Tom had turned on a spotlight and focused its powerful beam on me.

I have never been particularly religious, not in the sense that I went to church regularly or believed in a specific doctrine. But I do consider myself spiritual. I believe in a force beyond us, called God, and that our seeking and striving to understand that force adds meaning to life.

I also love coincidences, which I consider a first cousin of spirituality. I'm always trying to add significance to coincidences that other people tend to ignore. I believe both mystery and guidance is taking place when a phone call comes in just as I'm thinking about the person on the other end of the line, or when the perfect book falls off the shelf as I'm searching for answers to a problem, or when a train ride I normally don't take brings an old friend needing help back into my life. I pay attention to the small arbitrary links between other people and myself. It's one way I seek connection.

As I sat there in the pew, hearing Tom's remarks about

presidential sex lives and connecting it to my past, the coincidence overwhelmed me.

I knew at that moment that I would seek him out after the service and tell him my story. I needed to unburden myself completely. On most Sundays, after the service, while I was making tapes and labels and updating the church's website, Tom would stick his head in my office so that I could give him a thumbs-up or -down about the sales prospects of his talk (that Sunday's sermon immediately became our all-time bestselling audio). But that day he sensed something wrong with me, and we arranged a time to talk at the end of the day in his spacious seventh-floor office overlooking the church clock tower.

I started out by telling Tom how close to home his sermon had been for me. I didn't stumble over the next part. I used pretty much the same words with which I opened this book. I was eager to get everything off my chest.

Perhaps I needed him to tell me that I wasn't guilty of promiscuity way back when. Perhaps I needed him to help me connect the dots on why I was always searching for intimacy but had failed to find it. Perhaps I just needed some sanctioned spiritual authority figure to tell me that I was okay—and that I could forgive myself.

Tom didn't disappoint me. He was surprised but not dumbfounded by my story. He had heard many more painful stories over the years. He took my discomfort and held it up to God in prayer. He prayed that I would always be surrounded by God's grace and guidance as I dealt with this part of my life.

I realize now that each time I told the secret to someone I was getting one step closer to restoring my emotional health.

With Joan Ellis, I learned that the world wouldn't fall apart if I broke my promise to Tony.

With my sister Deb, who intuited the JFK relationship, I learned that maybe I was overestimating the shock value of my past and exaggerating the shame that other people would cast on me. My sister, for one, didn't see anything shameful in my secret.

With Marnie I got a vivid flashback to the girl I was back then in 1963 — a young woman sufficiently lively and winsome to attract the President of the United States. I had literally shuttered away and forgotten that young woman.

With K. C. Hyland, I got understanding.

With Tom Tewell, I received comfort, peace, even a sense of forgiveness. His exact words were, "There's more healing to be done here, and it will happen."

For the first time since JFK's death I was blessed with a feeling of grace and serenity. Why it happened then, I can't say for sure. Some feelings materialize within us, and their source is a mystery. The best explanation comes from a talk I had in 2010 while interviewing Dr. Evan Imber-Black, a therapist and authority on the power of secrets in families. She told me that my JFK secret had been at the heart of my marriage to Tony. In agreeing not to talk about it, the secret shaped how the two of us related to each other. It was a simple dynamic: We can't talk about *this,* so we can't talk about anything else that might possibly lead back to *it.* That's how silence entered the marriage and grew and never left. Now here I was nearly forty years later, breaking that silence without fear of reprisal — and knowing that it was a healing gesture.

That's the best explanation for the serenity I felt. My secret wasn't that big a deal anymore. I had outgrown it. It was part of who I was, but it didn't define me — and after talking with Dr. Tewell, it didn't restrict me. A burden had been not only lifted but discarded.

I knew what the poet Kim Rosen meant when she wrote, "When you welcome what you've been running from, your life is no longer shaped by trying to avoid it." My secret was not buried. It wasn't a secret at all. It was simply a fact from my past.

Chapter Fourteen

Whatever serenity I felt would be severely tested three years later by the New York *Daily News.*

I hope it's obvious, by this point, that I don't have any illusions about myself as some crucial, clandestine character in history. I know I am a footnote to history—no, strike that. I'm not even a footnote, because that would suggest that I had a role in the course of historical events that was consequential in some way, that had some impact on a conversation or a decision that affected the lives of others. That didn't happen. If anything, I'm a footnote to a footnote in the story of America's thirty-fifth president, someone so far off the radar that a diligent biographer couldn't identify me by my full name in his JFK biography.

But that began to change on Tuesday, May 13, when the *Daily News* ran a teaser item titled "Fun and Games with Mimi in the White House," linking the name to an intern's affair with JFK. The news item had no specific information connected to me, but I sensed they were closing in on the truth. In an earlier time I would have panicked and melted into a nervous puddle. But at this point my only concern was reaching my daughters, who were now in their thirties and married with children, so they could hear the truth from me rather than from the press.

I talked to Dr. Tewell the day the "Mimi" story appeared, and he had generously offered to pay for me to travel to Lisa in Virginia and Jenny in San Francisco. But I didn't believe I had enough time to do that. The *Daily News* already had my first name; it wouldn't be long before they found me.

Later that day I telephoned my daughters, haltingly articulating the string of words that I had carefully scripted in my head: When I was an intern in Washington in 1962 I had had an affair with President Kennedy. The relationship lasted for nearly eighteen months and, yes, I had told their father, although he and I never talked about it after November 22, 1963.

I'll always cherish their responses.

Lisa said, "Mom, I can't believe you were nineteen and you couldn't tell your own mother." She had immediately envisioned me as I was back then: young, naïve, vulnerable, and isolated by a secret, even from my parents.

Jenny asked, "What did it do to you to hide the truth for so long?" She had immediately focused on the burden I had carried.

With my daughters in the loop, I wasn't worried.

The next day I went to work. Nothing happened at first. No unusual phone calls, emails, or messages. Around noon, Dr. Tewell told me he was going to be away for a few days and had asked Associate Pastor Janice Smith Ammon to watch out for me, to step in should I need help. Jan and I had a wonderful talk later that afternoon about how this story might release something inside me and change my life in ways I couldn't imagine, for the better. I felt good. Although

I didn't relish the idea of being stalked by the press (who would?), I knew that telling the truth was not only my sole option but possibly my salvation.

I returned to my office on the church's first floor to find Celeste Katz, the *Daily News* reporter, waiting outside my door. She asked me point-blank if I was the Mimi who had been mentioned in the *News* article the day before.

"Yes, I am," I said.

I invited her to join me in the church sanctuary next to my office. I had a favorite seat in the ninth pew, so I guided her there. As we sat in the vast silent space, my serenity stayed with me. She asked me some basic fact-checking questions—my age, my job, my marital status, the year I graduated from Miss Porter's. I answered them calmly and asked her to leave. She asked if the paper could take a picture. I politely declined.

The remaining hours of that day were spent in a comical tango with the media. Jan alerted me that there was a *Daily News* photographer hanging around the church's side entrance on Fifty-fifth Street with orders to get a picture of me. So after some fumbling around for the key, she and I decided to unlock the church's massive front doors and exit where nobody would be expecting us: the main entrance on Fifth Avenue. We were holding hands as we ran down the steps and raced toward Madison Avenue to catch a bus to my apartment. We had to laugh at the ridiculousness of it all.

At my apartment building on Ninetieth Street, a brazen reporter from the *National Enquirer* had snuck in, gone up to the seventh floor, and knocked on my door, to no avail. He was stepping out of the elevator as Jan and I were stepping in. The door closed before he realized who we were, and we rode up to my apartment in peace. I called the superintendent, who escorted the reporter off the premises. Inside the apartment, the telephone began ringing and ringing, I let the calls fill up my answering machine — and privately noted that news travels fast.

Dr. Tewell had warned me that unless I was going to hold a press conference at my building — no, thank you — I should prepare a statement to keep the media at bay when the story broke. I wrote it and went over the wording on the phone with Tom and my daughters that evening.

> *From June 1962 to November 1963, I was involved in a sexual relationship with President Kennedy. For the last 41 years, it is a subject that I have not discussed. In view of the recent media coverage, I have now discussed the relationship with my children and my family, and they are completely supportive.*
>
> *I have no further comment on the subject. I would request that the media respect my privacy and the privacy of my family in the matter.*

I thought it was short and dignified, with enough specific information to feed the media beast. Tom preferred saying "love affair" rather than "sexual relationship," but I didn't want any ambiguity in the statement, which would only lead to follow-up questions. If I was going to be besieged by the press, I'd simply hand them the statement and be done with it.

The next morning, Thursday, May 15, I checked the *Daily News* online, and there was the front-page headline: "JFK Intern Admits All: City church worker, 60, says, 'I was the Mimi.'" I savored the peculiar locution of "the Mimi" — as if I were some kind of evil alien being. I called my building's super, who informed me that a flock of reporters was waiting for me on the street, including a camera crew from CNN. Jan came over, as we had arranged, to accompany me to work. After we emerged from the building, I handed out the statement and we jumped into a waiting taxi. As it pulled away, I saw Celeste Katz peer into my window, mouthing the words "I'm sorry." But she had nothing to be sorry for. Everything she wrote was accurate, and I was convinced she had done me a big favor.

The media nonsense was so much worse at the church—phones ringing, reporters pestering my colleagues as they showed up for work, seeking tidbits about me—that by noon we all agreed that I should return home, close the blinds, and ride the frenzy out.

So I did. I went home and committed myself to "house arrest" for as long as necessary.

My confinement wasn't unpleasant. My apartment was cozy and comfortable. I caught up on my reading and knitting. Friends brought me food and good company. I stayed in touch a few times a day with Lisa and Jenny. My gallant super guarded the front door of the building and reported on the whereabouts of reporters and photographers who hung out across the street. We wondered why they didn't leave. The super, who by now had developed a friendly but firm relationship with the reporters keeping me captive, told me that they thought I had somehow escaped through a back door and had been whisked off to New Jersey by a family member.

I received dozens of emails and letters from family members and friends. It was hard not to feel supported with messages like this on my computer: *I cried as I read the article in the Daily News. I cried because of your honesty, your courage, and maybe most of all your self-confidence. You are a wonderful per-*

son and have incredible strength. I am proud to be your friend. I love you very much.

Voicemail messages from reporters around the world and hand-delivered letters requesting TV interviews continued coming in.

I didn't respond to any requests—not even those from personal favorites, such as Katie Couric and Diane Sawyer. I trusted my inner voice which said, "Stay quiet. Stay peaceful. You are in charge here."

After five days, the reporters disappeared from the street below my apartment and it was safe to take a run in Central Park and do my own food shopping. The media requests slowed down to a trickle, and then they, too, stopped. Soon I was back to work, business as usual. I had survived.

My house arrest had been good for my emotions, my self-esteem, my state of mind, and my decision to not hide from the truth and yet maintain my privacy and dignity. And I savored how utterly unshaken I was about letting the secret out. My calm response to an event I had dreaded for years had been hard-earned. But your life can change overnight when you are the subject of tabloid headlines. And mine was about to change in a way I never dreamed of.

One of the letters I received was from a man named Richard Alford. Though his name sounded vaguely familiar, I couldn't remember anything about him, and I was certain I didn't know him. But when he read the story on the front page of the *Daily News,* he contacted me. This is what he wrote:

> *Dear Mimi,*
> *Since you are smart I'm sure you anticipated that your brief and to the point comment would bring a lot of*

exposure. As a friend I hope you stick to your statement
and just ride out the storm. I don't have to tell you that all
sorts of people will send you proposals for books, TV ap-
pearances (Larry King, Barbara Walters etc.), TV movies
etc. etc. I hope you don't need the money as a lot of money
will be mentioned up front. I would guess in the millions.
As a friend I hope you stick to your guns.

I have spent the last 7½ years in India and Tokyo
starting (in India) and running offices for IMG. Mark
McCormack the founder of IMG and a friend and boss
of mine died just hours ago having been in a coma for 4
months. All very sad . . . I live at 91ˢᵗ Street and Madison
and would love to see you when the dust settles (it always
does). If you have a question you would like friendly and
free advice on give me a call at home. I don't go to the of-
fice much.

Take care and good luck.

Dick

I didn't respond to his note. But his words made a distinct
impression in a couple of ways. For one thing, I appreciated
his shrewd warning about all the offers and big dollar num-
bers that would be tossed at me in the coming days. But
mostly I thought it was odd to receive such personal advice
from a stranger who took the liberty of referring to me as a
"friend." I didn't know the man. How could he say he knew
me? I filed it away with all the other letters.

I had turned sixty a week before the news broke. I had been
single and living alone in Manhattan for thirteen years. I had
been through an ultimately fruitless on-again, off-again rela-

tionship with a man for much of that time. I say ultimately fruitless because he was never the man I was hoping for: someone who shared my interests and with whom I knew, deep down, I could share my life forever. Our relationship continued from year to year largely on inertia, almost as if we hadn't noticed time slipping by. It fizzled out for good in 2002. I wasn't sad or discouraged. I was ticked off at myself for wasting so much time and having ignored how I really felt about our relationship. I wasn't getting any younger.

But I never gave up hope. I wanted what everyone wants: to love and be loved.

Friends suggested a Manhattan dating agency, but after paying the up-front fee of $2,500 and filling out my profile I noticed a serious flaw in their business model: *They* matched you up with the so-called right man and *they* determined whether or not you got to meet him—which took all of the control out of my hands and, let's face it, most of the fun, too. What good is broadcasting who you are and what you're looking for in a relationship if you can't sift through the responses and decide the next step by yourself? It's the most personal decision; no one should make it for you.

I knew the major online dating services offered more options, and I decided to post my profile on Match.com. I included the usual personal statistics, adding that my favorite movie is *Witness.* I ended by writing, "I'd love to be with a man who wants to cook together."

The act of writing a profile forced me to articulate what I was looking for in a man. I didn't find that fellow among the five men I met online. Each date was pleasant enough but featured an odd unexpected moment that I found off-putting. The first man, by sheer coincidence, had worked for an old friend of mine who had fired him. The man still harbored

sore feelings about it and voiced them persistently over dinner. I told him that I wouldn't tolerate hearing anything bad
said about someone I admired—or our date would be over.
Another date arrived two hours late at my office to pick me
up for dinner. I remember eagerly jumping into his car (perhaps because I was starving by then), enjoying our meal together, and just as eagerly jumping out when he drove me
home and invited himself up to my apartment. (No way was
that going to happen.) With each date I was learning to assert
myself and not settle for anyone who wasn't right for me.

My fifth and final date was the revelation. By then I had
learned the wisdom of beginning with a "coffee date," not
lunch or dinner. We met at a Greek diner. He was slim and
athletic, an avid biker. I could have overlooked his nervous
laugh and clammy handshake, but not the fact that he ordered three courses while I sipped my coffee. Even worse, he
spent the entire time talking about himself, which is surely
why, outside on the street, he told me what a great time he'd
had.

'Let's do this again," he said.

"Let's not," I said, and abruptly turned 180 degrees and
walked away.

When I turned the corner onto a side street, out of the
man's view, I felt exhilarated, pumping my fist as if I'd just
won a close, crucial point in tennis. (If I wore a hat, I probably would have tossed it into the air like the opening credits
of *The Mary Tyler Moore Show*.) Yes, I had been rude, but this
tiny act of self-assertion was a huge step forward for me. I
immediately dialed my sister Deb in Oregon on my cellphone to share the moment with her. She, more than anyone, understood how stifled and passive I had been with the
men in my life.

"You'll never believe what I just did. . . ." I told her, and then described the date note for note.

"Congratulations!" was all Deb could say. At that moment, I felt like someone should have handed me a diploma for finally being the person I wanted to be.

A few weeks later, the Dallek book and *Daily News* story splashed into my life and I removed my profile from the Internet.

Three months later on a warm Saturday afternoon in August, I was reading in my living room. August weekends in New York City are different from the rest of the year. The city is blazing in pavement-melting heat. The streets are eerily quiet because a lot of people have left town for the weekend. I often visited my married friends in Connecticut on such days, but on this weekend I had decided to stay home. Being alone was therapeutic; for years I kept an old-fashioned steno pad next to my favorite overstuffed chair, jotting down thoughts and making lists of things to do—endless lists. Fall was around the corner. What did I want to do? How did I see my life unfolding? What were my goals? These were my questions that Saturday afternoon. I reached for the steno pad to start writing when a thought, almost like a voice, entered my head. Perhaps being home alone reminded me of the enforced solitude I had enjoyed after the *Daily News* piece. Perhaps I wanted to recapture the self-confident feelings that I had handled everything so well. Whatever it was, I was drawn to the file drawer in my closet and pulled out the folder on all that had happened in May. There was the note from Dick Alford.

I sat down at my desk and wrote to him. Ten days later he

answered and said he would give me a call in mid-September when he returned from a two-week trip. When we spoke on the phone, I suggested my standard first-date ploy—a cup of coffee—but Dick convinced me that he was interesting enough to risk a full meal.

Although he claimed to know me, I didn't recognize him when we met for dinner at a neighborhood restaurant halfway between his apartment and mine. My first impression was positive. He was my height. He had chiseled facial features, silvery blue eyes, and bushy, professorial eyebrows. Despite his stark white hair, he had a vigorous, athletic spring in his step. Plus, he held the door for me as I entered the restaurant: always a good sign.

We started with small talk, amazed that we had lived two blocks apart and had never noticed each other on the street or at an ATM or a grocery store. Dick explained that for the past eight years he had been living and working in India and Japan, returning to New York only for vacations. But he was back for good now. I learned that he had been divorced for nearly thirty years, that he had two grown children, and that we had many friends and interests in common. We had both been marathon runners, loved New York City and the country, and regarded Central Park as a sacred civic shrine.

The similarities didn't stop there. I learned that, like Tony, Dick was a graduate of Williams College and Harvard Business School. Also like Tony, his first job out of college was at Morgan Guaranty. Although Dick had not been in the same class or a close friend, he had known Tony and remembered seeing us at parties on the Upper East Side in the mid-1970s. He had spent most of his career in sports marketing and, for several years, had worked on developing corporate sponsorships for the New York City Marathon and a race

called the Fifth Avenue Mile. That's how he had met me in
the early 1980s at the New York Road Runners Club offices
when I worked there. I liked that he remembered me, although I struggled in vain to recall meeting him—a fact that
did not seem to faze him.

Then something clicked that brought me closer to Dick.
I recalled a small coincidence that happened back in May.
Dick had written his note to me on the day his boss and
friend of forty years, Mark McCormack, had died. If I didn't
remember Dick's face, at least I remembered his boss's name.
A week after receiving Dick's note, on the first day I returned
to work after my "house arrest," Dr. Tewell had come into my
office to discuss the audio taping of a memorial service to be
held later that morning in the sanctuary. It stood out because
Arnold Palmer and Jean-Claude Killy—big sports stars for
my generation—would be giving eulogies and the great so-
prano Renée Fleming would be singing Schubert's "Ave
Maria." The memorial service was for Dick's boss. It occurred
to me that Dick must have been in the church that day while
I was overseeing the taping.

It was a slender strand of synchronicity, to be sure, but it
was enough to convince me that this would not be our first
and only dinner together.

On our second dinner date, we made a seemingly silly
connection over Brussels sprouts. Dick announced that they
were his favorite vegetable. It's possible that was the moment
I felt the first stirrings of love for him. What could be better,
I thought, than a man whose enthusiasm for Brussels sprouts
matched mine?

Soon we were seeing each other two or three times a
week. We walked and talked to exhaustion in Central Park.
We traded memories about races that we might have un-

knowingly been in together. He told me how in the 1970s as a divorced single father he would pick up his two very young children in Delaware, drive back to New York City for the weekend with them, and spend endless hours in the park. He showed me the rocks at the park's north end where he taught them to rock-climb. He reminisced about taking care of his kids—one in diapers—all by himself, fearing he couldn't pull it off, and then pulling it off. I saw a sensitive, responsible, loving man and I liked what I saw. He seemed to want to tell me everything about himself, but he was also cautious about not coming on too strong.

One evening Dick arrived at my apartment armed with pots, pans, and all the ingredients, including spices, to prepare dinner for us. A guy who cooks is good, I thought— actually, better than good. As he worked on the meal, he sheepishly explained a hidden self-interest in all his effort. He had gone on the South Beach Diet to lose a few pounds to impress me and wanted to make sure he stuck to the diet's guidelines.

Recalling what I wrote about cooking together at the end of my online dating profile, I began to suspect that I had met an uncanny match in Dick.

Despite all the time we spent together, it wasn't a whirlwind courtship. It was cautious, polite, perhaps even languorous. We had been dating nine months before Dick invited me to his country home in the Berkshires of Massachusetts in a tiny town named Alford (no relation, just coincidence). Dick had made titanic preparations for that weekend in early May 2004, intent on showing me a great time in a part of the world he loved. It was also my sixty-first birthday. He orchestrated everything: sights, events, shops, meals, wines, even the videos we would watch at night. By the second day I was not only exhausted but distressed. I felt that Dick was so absorbed in dazzling me that he forgot about how I was feeling. We weren't connecting. We were checking off a list of weekend things to do but not sharing the most simple emotional and physical contact—which is all I really wanted. Everything else was "nice to have," not "must have."

Over breakfast I described my concerns.

I was stunned by his response. He didn't just raise his voice. He went on an angry, red-faced tirade, lashing out at me for not appreciating all the effort he had made, mocking me for being so negative.

I was familiar with this kind of rage and bullying from my marriage. But this time I wasn't going to put up with it. I would rather be alone than compromise on what I wanted in a relationship. I had made mistakes and I had learned from them, and I was simply not going to repeat them.

So I packed my bag and took the next train home. I sat immobile all the way to New York, alternating between staring straight ahead and breaking down in tears. Mercifully, it was still early in the day and the car was empty; there were no passengers who had to endure my sobbing.

I was certain that things were over between Dick and me. But he called a week later, which impelled me to write him a letter using the convenient phrasing that I was "sad our relationship didn't work out." Then I took it further and explained what had been missing from the weekend. It was simple: Even though we were having a nice time, Dick was operating at a remove from me. At the most basic level, I needed to hear from him how he felt about being with me. He could have done that with a word, a touch, a glance, a joke. But he didn't. And it upset me. I was through with those kinds of relationships.

After he read my letter, he called again, claiming that he
wanted to know exactly how I defined a healthy relationship.
This touchy-feely stuff was all new to him, and he wanted to
do better. We agreed to discuss it over coffee at the Starbucks
on Eighty-seventh Street and Lexington Avenue. He was sitting at a window table when I arrived. I was eager to see him,
but also cautious. I didn't hug or kiss him before I sat down.
Again, I described what I expected from him when he was
with me. I was trying to be clear about my needs for emotional and physical affection and the kind of simple, loving,
spontaneous attention that defined a strong, intimate partnership for me. I could give that to him, but I expected it
back in return. More than anything, I expected complete
honesty from him. That didn't mean he had to overshare
about every detail. It simply meant that in the space that held
us together, there would be no secrets. Anything less would
be dishonest. I had spent my entire life misguidedly cradling
a secret and letting it close off, one by one, the doors to my
heart. I wasn't going to make that mistake again.

I could tell by his anguished expression that Dick was
struggling with my explanation. No one, he admitted, had
ever talked to him this way. But I was heartened by it as well.
Struggling meant he was listening.

We parted with no promise to see each other again. I
walked north back to my apartment, replaying my words and
feeling satisfied that I had taken control and asserted my
feelings about a relationship with a man on my terms.

Dick got on the subway at Eighty-sixth Street, heading
south for a summer solstice party at the other end of Manhattan. Then he did the most remarkable thing. At the next
stop, he got out of the subway and ran up the stairs to the
street. He was trying to remember everything I said and
wanted to write it down. But he didn't have a pen. He bought

one on the street and recorded his notes on scraps of paper in his pocket.

I think I sensed that as I walked back to my apartment. I had finally met a man who didn't belittle my needs, who dignified them by being open to the possibility of change in himself.

We started seeing each other again soon after. If there was an "electric" moment when we both knew we had found "the one" in each other, it had to be sitting on the park bench at Ninetieth Street and Fifth Avenue, beneath the statue of Fred Lebow, my late boss and the founder of the New York Road Runners Club. We both knew Fred. The statue depicts Fred looking at his watch, timing a runner. But Dick and I were thinking the same thing—that Fred was really telling us, "It's about time."

On October 2, 2005, Dick and I were married in Alford, Massachusetts. I was sixty-three, he was sixty-seven. We gave up our apartments in New York and now live in retirement in a small house in the country. We share a life that is filled with long walks and bike rides, cooking and gardening, culture and travel, lots of family and friends, and a love that keeps growing.

Our marriage is what I like to call a "mundane adventure." We find a way to take the common rituals of everyday life and somehow brighten them up.

Even the simple requirements of living on a fixed income have their moments. We have a weekly ritual we call "Fridays" when Dick and I review every penny we spent the previous week—from the $26 to fill up the gas tank to the $10.50 matinee at the Triplex to $307.25 for an insurance premium. We add up the totals, split it fifty-fifty, and reimburse the week's big spender to break even. Occasionally, one of us will highlight an item that only one of us needed or enjoyed—and deduct it from the total. It's a small gesture, but it reminds me that even in our household budgeting sessions we have found a way of giving each other a gift.

I no longer have to bring Dick up to speed on how to act in a relationship with me. Quite often, he's the one offering me sweet teachable moments. One morning he was making breakfast for us, sliding strips of bacon into a brand-new skillet. I mentioned that he had the heat too high.

He calmly turned around and said, "Mimi, sometimes I need to make my own mistakes."

He was right, of course.

Another time, again over breakfast, two years into our marriage, Dick stared into my eyes and in a deadpan tone as dry as desert sand said, "Mimi, when I married you I thought I had won the perfect woman. But now that I've been living with you for a few years, I realize you have a lot of issues and faults."

I had to reciprocate. I took Dick's hands and said, "I know what you mean. When we first met, I thought you had a lot of deep-seated issues. I didn't know if this thing of ours would work. But now that we've been together for a while, I have to admit it: You're perfect!"

We laughed. Neither of us is perfect, but we're perfect together.

I know I'm gushing over my husband and my marriage, but I do so as an object lesson in how we find happiness when we least expect it—if we know how to look for it and to fight for it. I say this because I think I deserve as much credit for my current healthy state of mind as anyone. I didn't just meet a man who loved me. I met a man who led me to understand myself.

———

In early 2011, Dick and I had rented a house in West Palm Beach, Florida, to escape a brutal winter in Alford. Our friend Mark was visiting one weekend when Dick noticed that a professional golf tournament was being played twenty minutes away in Boca Raton—and to his delight, admission was free. How could the three of us pass this up?

We jumped in the car and headed to the tournament. Dick was behind the wheel. As we neared the event, there was some confusion about where to park. Dick passed one parking lot and then another and then another, seemingly oblivious to the fact that he was taking us farther and farther away from the tournament entrance. Mark turned to me and asked, "Doesn't this drive you crazy?"

"Not at all," I told him, "I don't let little things like this ruin my day. Being happy is more important than being right about where to park."

"That's very enlightened," he said.

I realized he was right—and saw how far I'd come. What seemed so simple to achieve now—happiness in the moment and with a fine man—appeared like personal enlightenment to an outside observer.

I'm no longer the passive, silent wife and mother. I have a voice. And part of being happy is using that voice to speak up for yourself at the moments when your emotional well-being is at risk, and staying quiet when it doesn't matter. If Dick wanted to fumble around the neighborhood, looking for a parking spot miles from the golf course, what did it really matter in the grand scheme of things? There would be a shuttle bus to take us to the gate. We would be together the whole time.

I know I'm happy. But what's even more amazing is that the positive spirit I feel on the inside shows on the outside. My sister Deb sees it most plainly—and with the greatest satisfaction. Dick and I were driving around Bainbridge Island in Seattle with Deb and her husband, Perry. The car was filled with good vibes and silly laughter. We were having a great time when Deb exclaimed, "Oh, Dick, it's wonderful that you are with Mimi. It's so much fun to be with the two of you. You deserve the coin."

I had no idea what she was talking about. "What coin?" I asked.

Deb explained that sometime during the late 1990s, she was driving in Northern California when I called her on her cellphone from New York for some much-needed sisterly support. We had these coast-to-coast talks often and they always cheered me up. On this occasion I was more teary-eyed and sad than usual, wondering if I would ever be really happy. Deb pulled off the road into a deserted parking lot so we could talk more. After we hung up, she stepped out of the car to stretch her legs and there on the ground, shining in the sunlight, was a Kennedy half-dollar coin. She picked it up and told herself, "I'm keeping this coin to give to the man who makes my sister happy."

"You're kidding," I said. "You never told me this."

Two days after we returned from Seattle, a package arrived for Dick. It was a small heart-shaped box, and in it was a Kennedy half-dollar. Deb's note said: "Dear Dick. Enclosed as promised. Thank you for making Mimi so happy."

I rarely think of JFK today. But now it's by personal choice, not by someone's edict. However, I still tear up when I see a picture of him, and sometimes there's a catch in my voice when I talk about him. The memories of my time with him mix with images of his horrific death and with the emotional trauma I went through the day he died, and I'm hurtled back to being that nineteen-year-old woman again. That will probably never change.

I want to talk to that young woman, but I'm not sure I have anything profound to say or even if she would listen to me. I'm not sure that I could counsel her properly on what to do with her secret about JFK, or how to take control of her own story. I'm not sure that revealing it to family and friends would have changed her life or saved her marriage or released her from her emotional shell or brought her decades of uninterrupted contentment. It might have altered the course of her life. It might not.

I've always wondered if the years of confusion and doubt were worth it. To that question I can only answer a resounding yes. Because they made me who I am today. I am proof that if we're lucky, we emerge from our mistakes as wiser, stronger, better people—and if we're extremely lucky, happier people.

I think back to that pivotal moment over coffee when I outlined to Dick what I was looking for in a relationship. What I remember most clearly is how intently he was listening to me. When someone listens to you, they may not realize it but they're giving you a great gift: They're making room for your voice. That's what the contentment in my marriage has given me: a voice. That's why I'm able to write these words, and this book.

In January 2009, Dick and I traveled to Washington, D.C., to visit JFK's grave at Arlington National Cemetery. I'd never seen the site before and was curious to see what emotions and memories a visit might inspire. Well, curious and afraid, too.

It was eight degrees without the windchill as we trudged through the snow to the modest grave site at the bottom of a hill below the grand Greek revival Arlington House, the city of Washington spread out before us. JFK's flat headstone rests next to that of Jacqueline Bouvier Kennedy Onassis. Even if it hadn't been so bone-chillingly cold, I wouldn't have lingered at his grave. As I contemplated the scene, I felt like an intruder. The Kennedy legacy had hovered over my life in a silent, pernicious way for a long time, but I had never really been part of the story. As I say, I was a footnote to a footnote. And as I stood there, snuggling up to my husband to keep warm, my arm tucked under his, I was perfectly fine with that.

Just before leaving, I silently mouthed the words "Thank you" in gratitude and amazement at how my secret, the source of so much of my pain, turned out to be my life's redeeming force. Without the secret and its public revelation, I would never have met Dick, or found the life I have today. Whatever memories I had of JFK were in the past, where they belonged and where they would stay. The only thing that mattered was that, at long last, I was at peace.

That's a secret I am happy to let go of and share.

Acknowledgments

My heartfelt thanks to the following:

My agent and friend, Mark Reiter, for helping me transform my story into a book.

My support squad of friends: Marnie Pillsbury, Wendy Foulke, Kirk Huffard, K. C. Hyland, and Joan Ellis, for sharing their memories; Mary Hilliard, for her fabulous photograph.

My siblings: Deb Beardsley, Buffy Havard, Josh Beardsley, and Jim Beardsley, for their unconditional support.

My daughters: Lisa Alpaugh and Jenny Axelman, for standing by me and accepting that this was the story I needed to tell.

Colette Linnihan, for her guidance and expertise in helping me to understand.

Jude Elliot Mead and Rebecca Busselle, for their early encouragement; and Linda Bird Francke, for her time and contribution.

My teammates at Random House: Susan Mercandetti, for giving this book a home; Susan Kamil and Andy Ward, for the most intense and thoughtful scrutiny an author's words could ever receive; and Ben Steinberg and Kaela Myers, for their positive attitudes and prompt attention that never failed me.

My beloved husband, Dick Alford, for endless rereadings, making me laugh, soothing my tears, and welcoming me with open arms no matter what. I am so happy to be sharing the rest of my life with you.

ABOUT THE AUTHOR

<small>MIMI ALFORD</small> lives in western Massachusetts with her husband, Dick. Together they have seven grandchildren. This is her first book.

ABOUT THE TYPE

This book was set in Linotype Didot, a modern adaptation of Firmin Didot's original 1784 design, then called French Modern Face Didot. Considered to be an elegant, neoclassical typeface, it was redrawn in 1991 by Adrain Frutiger for the Linotype foundry to address the demands of legibility in digital typesetting.